CHUNKY KNITS

31 PROJECTS FOR YOU & YOUR HOME
KNIT WITH BULKY YARN

ASHLEY LITTLE

LARK

Editor
Beth Sweet

Art Director & Cover Designer
Carol Barnao

Illustrator
Orrin Lundgren

Photographer
Cynthia Shaffer

LARK CRAFTS

An Imprint of Sterling Publishing
387 Park Avenue South
New York, NY 10016

ISBN 978-1-4547-0871-1

Distributed in Canada by Sterling Publishing
c/o Canadian Manda Group, 165 Dufferin Street
Toronto, Ontario, Canada M6K 3H6
Distributed in the United Kingdom by GMC Distribution Services
Castle Place, 166 High Street, Lewes, East Sussex, England BN7 1XU
Distributed in Australia by Capricorn Link (Australia) Pty. Ltd.
P.O. Box 704, Windsor, NSW 2756, Australia

For information about custom editions, special sales, and premium and corporate purchases,
please contact Sterling Special Sales at 800-805-5489 or specialsales@sterlingpublishing.com.

Email academic@larkbooks.com for information about desk and examination copies.
The complete policy can be found at larkcrafts.com.

Every effort has been made to ensure that all the information in this book is accurate. However,
due to differing conditions, tools, and individual skills, the publisher cannot be responsible for any
injuries, losses, and other damages that may result from the use of the information in this book.

Manufactured in China

2 4 6 8 10 9 7 5 3 1

larkcrafts.com

CONTENTS

INTRODUCTION

Are you a yarn fanatic? It's okay to admit it.

When I go to a yarn store, I love to explore every skein of yarn and feel it squish between my fingers. Sometimes I imagine what it would feel like to wear the yarn as a sweater. In all my years of knitting, I've found that chunky yarns are some of the most satisfying.

Bulky and super-bulky weights are notorious for being cheater yarns — yarns that don't take much time to knit up. But what's wrong with being quick and convenient?

In my dream world, my stash would be just as gorgeous as any yarn store's stock, organized by weight and color, of course. Chunky yarns are the skeins I pick up and buy for no reason other than the fact that I'm incredibly drawn to them. They're the yarns that are never quite perfect for the new wrap I want to knit or for the pair of gloves I was going to give my friend. "Oh, no," I say to the yarn. "You're not right for this pattern." Then I give that skein a few loving pats and place it back on the shelf.

The truth is that I love the yarn so much, I can't bear the thought of parting with it, especially when I'm giving it away as a gift.

It's true in some cases that I could just go and buy more yarn, but most of my chunky yarn stash is filled with discontinued colors and skeins from random shops I may never have an opportunity to return to. These are the yarns I keep on the shelf, the ones I never want to use because no pattern is deemed quite good enough for them.

And then the opportunity to write *Chunky Knits* came along. As the gorgeous samples rolled in from the contributors, I matched them to yarns in my stash. Yes, yes, that cobalt blue bulky yarn would look fantastic as a Gothic Lace Wrap. A pair of gray Cozy Cable Mittens knitted with the yarn I bought in Paris? Yes, please. I found all the patterns worthy of de-stashing, adding enough projects to my to-knit list to keep me busy for the next three years.

Check out your stash and I'm sure you'll have a few skeins of bulky or super bulky yarn that are perfect for these projects. Better yet, I hope you discover some new favorites with the help of the contributors who designed these patterns with bulky and super-bulky yarn in mind. A lot of the projects make great gifts — and I promise not to tell if you don't use your absolute favorite chunky yarn for those projects.

BUTTON-UP SLOUCHY HAT

The look of this soft slouch changes instantly depending on the type of buttons you use. In addition to natural wooden buttons, you might want to play around with contrasting acrylics, filigreed brass, or even fabric-covered versions. If you're knitting this for a guy, you can omit the buttons for a more masculine style.

Skill Level: Easy   Design by: Amanda Lilley

MATERIALS AND TOOLS
- Berroco Vintage Chunky (50% acrylic, 40% wool, 10% nylon; 3.5oz/100g = 130yds/119m); 1 skein, Dungaree #6187– approximately 130yds/119m of bulky weight yarn ⑤
- Knitting needles: 5.5mm (size 9 U.S.) circular needle, 16"/41cm long and double pointed needles or size to obtain gauge
- 4 buttons, ¾"/2cm in diameter
- Stitch marker
- Tapestry needle

GAUGE
- 15 sts/18 rows = 4"/10cm in St st

FINISHED MEASUREMENTS
- 20"/51cm circumference, to fit 20–23"/51–58cm head circumference

instructions

GARTER STITCH BAND

Note: Sl first st of each row pwise wyif.

With circular needle, CO 84 sts. Do not join in the round.

Rows 1–4: Knit.

Row 5: K to last 9 sts, yo, k2tog, k2, k2tog, yo, k3.

Rows 6–16: Knit.

Row 17: Rep row 5.

Rows 18–20: Knit.

Row 21: K to last 12 sts. BO 12 sts—72 sts.

Break yarn.

BODY

Hold garter band with buttonholes on the left. Join yarn to top right side corner of the garter band.

Knit across 72 sts on needle. Pm and join to work in the round, being careful not to twist sts.

K in the rnd until hat measures 9"/23cm from CO edge.

SHAPE CROWN

Note: Change to dpns when needed.

Next (dec) rnd: *K6, k2tog, rep from * around—63 sts.

Knit 1 rnd.

Next (dec) rnd: *K5, k2tog, rep from * around—54 sts.

Knit 1 rnd.

Next (dec) rnd: *K4, k2tog, rep from * around—45 sts.

Next (dec) rnd: *K3, k2tog, rep from * around—36 sts.

Next (dec) rnd: *K2tog, rep from * around—18 sts.

Next (dec) rnd: *K2tog, rep from * around—9 sts.

FINISHING

Cut yarn and draw tail through remaining sts. Weave in all ends.

BOBBLE COWL

Your favorite cold-weather accessory is getting a makeover! It's a party every day when you upgrade to these fun, easy bobbles.

Skill Level: Intermediate

Design by: Meredith Crawford

MATERIALS AND TOOLS

- Berroco Weekend Chunky (75% Acrylic, 25% Peruvian Cotton; 3.5oz/100g = 119yds/109m); 4 skeins, color Pebble #6904—approximately 476yds/436m of bulky weight yarn (5)
- Knitting needles: 9mm (size 13 U.S.) circular needles, 16"/41cm long or size to obtain gauge
- Stitch markers
- Tapestry needle

GAUGE

- 12 sts/12 rows = 4"/10cm in bobble stitch pattern with 2 strands held tog

SPECIAL ABBREVIATION

- MB (Make Bobble): (K1, p1, k1) in the next st, turn, p3, turn, k3, turn, p3, turn, k3tog

FINISHED MEASUREMENTS

- 28" circumference x 12" tall (71cm x 30.5cm)

instructions

Holding 2 strands of yarn tog, CO 78 sts. Pm and join to work in the rnd, being careful not to twist sts.

Rnds 1-2: Purl.

Rnds 3-4: Knit.

Rnd 5: K1, *MB, k5; rep from * around until there are 5 sts left on needle, MB, k4.

Rnds 6-9: Knit.

Rnd 10: K4, *MB, k5; rep from * around to last st, k.

Rnds 11-14: Knit.

Rep rnds 5-14 twice, then rep rnd 5 once more.

Next 2 rnds: Knit.

Next 2 rnds: Purl.

BO pwise.

FINISHING

Weave in all ends.

JAR COZIES

Most of us have spare Mason jars hanging around the kitchen, just waiting for a creative outlet. Dress them up with these easy knitted covers in an array of colors, and use them to store pencils, knitting needles, your vintage button stash, or a bunch of sweet dried flowers. You can even pop a tea candle inside to add soft, flickering light to any room.

Skill Level: Easy   Design by: Megan Mannell

MATERIALS AND TOOLS

- Berroco Vintage Chunky (50% acrylic, 40% wool, 10% nylon; 3.5oz/100g = 130yds/119m); 1 skein each of Dried Plum #6180, Dewberry #6167, and Petunia #61105—approximately 15yds/14m of bulky weight yarn for the small cover, 24yds/22m for the medium cover, and 30yds/27m for the large cover (5)

- Knitting needles: 6mm (size 10 U.S.) double pointed needles or size to obtain gauge

- Stitch marker

- Craft glue

- Tapestry needle

GAUGE

- 12 sts/14 rows = 4"/10cm in pattern stitch

FINISHED MEASUREMENTS

- Small (half-pint jar): approx. 4"/10cm in height

- Medium (pint jar): approx. 5"/13cm in height

- Large (quart jar): approx. 7"/18cm in height

instructions

CO 20 (24, 28), leaving at least a 1yd/.9m tail. Pm and join to work in the rnd, being careful not to twist sts.

Rnd 1: Knit around.

Rnd 2: K4, *yo, k2tog, k2; rep from * around, yo.

Rnd 3: K2tog, k around—20 (24, 28) sts.

Rep Rnds 2 and 3 until piece measures approx. 3½ (5, 7½)"/9 (13, 19)cm in length.

Dec Rnd: *K2, k2tog, rep from *, around—15 (18, 21) sts.

BO tightly.

FINISHING

Weave in BO end only, leaving CO tail for securing cover to jar. Block cover gently by hand.

SECURING COVERS TO JARS

Pull the CO edge of your cover over the bottom of the jar. Pull the cover upward so that the CO edge is just underneath the top rim of the jar.

Optional step for half-pint jars: The pint and quart-size covers stay on very well due to the shape of the jars. For half-pint jars, however, you may want to secure covers with a small dot

of craft glue in 3 to 4 spots around the top of the jar. Pull the cover up over these glue dots and hold in place for about 60 seconds.

With tapestry needle and 1-yd/.9m tail you left on your CO edge, whipstitch (page 120) into each st on the CO edge.

Once you have drawn the tail through all the CO sts, pull taut and begin wrapping the tail tightly around the top of the jar, just under the rim where the lid screws on. Make sure you are wrapping over the CO edge of your cover.

With tapestry needle, thread the tail under your previous wraps. Tuck in the tail end by threading it under the cover's sts. Trim any excess tail that remains.

HONEYCOMB THROW

HONEYCOMB THROW

The luxurious drape and cuddly texture of this throw makes it extra cozy on chilly days (and a perfect accent for any room all year long). If you'd like to make a larger blanket, just buy extra yarn and work additional rows of the Honeycomb Stitch until you've reached the desired length.

Skill Level: Easy

Design by: Ashley Little

MATERIALS AND TOOLS

- Paton's Beehive Baby Chunky (70% acrylic, 30% nylon; 3.5oz/100g = 120yds/110m); 6 skeins, color Swifter Sea—approximately 720yds/658m of bulky weight yarn (5)
- Knitting needles: 8mm (size 11 U.S.) circular needle, 32"/81cm long or size to obtain gauge
- Cable needle
- Tapestry needle

GAUGE

- 16 sts/16 rows = 4"/10cm in Honeycomb Stitch

SPECIAL ABBREVIATIONS

- C4B: Sl 2 sts to cable needle and hold to back, k2, k2 from cable needle
- C4F: Sl 2 sts to cable needle and hold to front, k2, k2 from cable needle

SPECIAL STITCH

- Honeycomb Stitch: Worked over multiple of 8 sts
  Row 1: *C4B, C4F; repeat from * across.
  Rows 2 and 4: Purl.
  Row 3: Knit.
  Row 5: *C4F, C4B; repeat from * across.
  Rep Rows 2–4.

FINISHED MEASUREMENTS

- 34" long x 42" wide (86cm x 107cm)

instructions

CO 142 sts.

Rows 1–8: Work in seed st.

Row 9: Work first 7 sts in seed st, k to last 7 sts. Work rem sts in seed st.

Row 10: Work first 7 sts in seed st, p to last 7 sts. Work rem sts in seed st.

Row 11: Begin working Honeycomb Stitch, continuing to work the first and last 7 sts of each row in seed st for border. Cont until piece measures approximately 28"/71.12cm long, ending on Row 1 of the Honeycomb Stitch.

Next row: Rep Row 10

Next row: Rep Row 9.

Work in seed st for 8 rows. BO.

FINISHING

Weave in all ends.

BOOT CUFFS

Forget the boots-and-legwarmers combo that makes your legs feel somewhere between toasty and sweaty. These small cuffs sit at the top of your boot. They are knit flat and then seamed, so you can easily adjust them to fit your calf.

Skill Level: Easy   Design by: Mindy Lewis

MATERIALS AND TOOLS
- Lion Brand Wool-Ease Thick & Quick (80% acrylic, 20% wool; 5oz/142g = 106yds/97m); 2 skeins, color Fisherman #640-099—approximately 212yds/194m of super bulky weight yarn (6)
- Knitting needles: 9mm (size 13 U.S.) or size to obtain gauge
- Cable needle
- Tapestry needle

GAUGE
- 12 sts/14 rows = 4"/10cm over Cable Stitch pattern

SPECIAL ABBREVIATIONS
- C4F = Slip 2 sts to cable needle and hold at front of work, k2, k2 from cable needle
- C4B = Slip 2 sts to cable needle and hold at back of work, k2, k2 from cable needle

FINISHED MEASUREMENTS
- 13"/33cm circumference at widest point; 8½"/22cm long

instructions

(Make 2)

CO 24 sts.

Rows 1 and 3: K2, p2, k8, p2, k10.

Rows 2 and 4: K12, p8, k4.

Row 5: K2, p2, C4F, C4B, p2, k10.

Row 6: Rep row 2.

Rep these 6 rows nine times or until desired length to go around calf is reached.

BO.

FINISHING

Using mattress stitch (page 119), sew CO edge to BO edge.

Weave in all ends.

GOLDENROD COWL

The stitches in this pattern are perfect for highlighting a super bulky yarn. All those yarn-overs and elongated knit stitches that stretch over two rows create an unbelievably beautiful effect. If you're not a fan of sewing on buttons, trade them for a skewer or brooch. There's even an option to turn this cowl into a scarf.

Skill Level: Intermediate   Design by: Brenda Lavell

MATERIALS AND TOOLS

- Cascade Magnum (100% Peruvian Highland Wool; 8.82oz/250g = 123yds/112m); 1 skein, color Gold #9463B—approximately 123yds/112m of super bulky weight yarn (6)

- Knitting needles: 12mm (size 17 U.S.)

- Tapestry needle or crochet hook

- Two buttons, 2"/50mm in diameter (optional)

- Sewing needle and thread in color complementary to yarn and button color

GAUGE

- 8.5 sts/9 rows = 4"/10cm in St st, unblocked

SPECIAL ABBREVIATIONS

- s2k3p: slip 2, knit 3 together, pass the 2 slip stitches over the knit 3 together; 3 stitches decreased

FINISHED MEASUREMENTS

- 40" long x 10" deep (102cm x 25cm)

instructions

Note: Slip all stitches purlwise with yarn in front. CO 21 sts.

Row 1 (RS): K1, sl1, k2, *k1, yo; rep from * to last 4 sts. K2, sl1, k1.

Row 2 (WS): Sl1, p1, sl1, k1, *drop yo from previous row, k1; rep from * to last 4 sts, k1, sl1, p1, sl1.

Row 3: K1, sl1, k2, k3tog, [yo] twice, k1, [yo] twice, s2k3p, [yo] twice, k1, [yo] twice, k3tog, k2, sl1, k1.

Row 4: Sl1, p1, sl1, k1, *k1, [k1, k1 tbl] in same double yo; rep from * to last 6 sts, k3, sl1, p1, sl1.

Rows 5 and 6: Rep rows 1 and 2.

Row 7: K1, sl1, k2, *k1, [yo] twice, s2k3p, [yo] twice; rep from * to last 5 sts, k3, sl1, k1.

Row 8: Rep row 4.

Work Chart nine more times for a total of 10 repeats.

COWL EDGE

Work Rows 1–6 of Chart.

Next row (RS): K1, sl1, knit to last 2 sts, sl1, k1.

Next row (WS): Sl1, k1, sl1, knit to last 3 sts, sl1, k1, sl1.

Last row (RS): K2, transfer both sts back to LH needle, k2tog tbl, *k1, transfer with the previously ktog st back to LH needle and k2tog tbl; rep from * to end, using tapestry needle to draw yarn through final k2tog st.

FINISHING

Weave in ends. Block (page 120). Trim ends.

Space buttons evenly along BO edge, ensuring that the buttons slip neatly into the eyelets formed by the stitch pattern on the CO edge. Sew buttons into place.

Scarf option: With an additional 1–2 skeins of yarn, work repeats of rows 1–8 until desired length is reached. Work end as written for Cowl Edge.

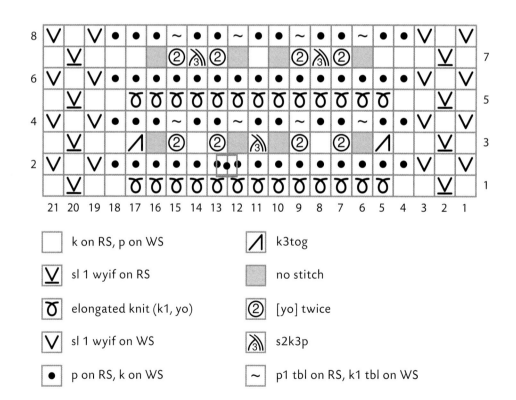

	k on RS, p on WS		k3tog
	sl 1 wyif on RS		no stitch
	elongated knit (k1, yo)	②	[yo] twice
	sl 1 wyif on WS		s2k3p
•	p on RS, k on WS	~	p1 tbl on RS, k1 tbl on WS

HERRINGBONE
TOTE

If you've ever wanted to try out the herringbone stitch, now's your chance. The shape of this little tote is inspired by 1940s bags and is knit in a tight gauge to make sure nothing important falls through the stitches. If you'd like, choose a pretty patterned fabric to line the tote's interior, giving it extra sturdiness and a pop of lovely color every time you reach inside.

Skill Level: Easy   Design by: Joleen Kraft

MATERIALS AND TOOLS

- Lion Brand Wool-Ease Thick & Quick (80% acrylic, 20% wool; 6oz/170g = 106yds/97m); 2 skeins, color Grass #640-131—approximately 212yds/194m of super bulky weight yarn (6)

- Knitting needles: 12mm (size 17 U.S.) or size to obtain gauge; 8mm (size 11 U.S.)

- Crochet hook: 6mm (size J-10 U.S.)

- 2 belts for bag handles

- Optional fabric for lining: 15"/38cm x 19"/48cm

GAUGE

- 12 sts/10 rows = 4"/10cm

SPECIAL ABBREVIATIONS

- HBK (herringbone knit RS): k2tog tbl and drop only first st off needle. Rep to last st, k1 tbl.

- HBP (herringbone purl WS): p2tog and drop only first st off needle. Rep to last st, p.

FINISHED MEASUREMENTS

- 14" wide x 9" deep (36cm x 23cm)

instructions

BAG PANEL (MAKE 2)

With larger needles, CO 40 sts.

Rows 1–9: Work HBK across odd rows and work HBP across even rows.

Row 10 (dec): P2tog, work HBP to last 2 sts, p2tog—38 sts.

Rows 11, 13, and 15 (dec): K2tog, work HBK to last 2 sts, k2tog—2 sts dec.

Rows 12 and 14: HBP across.

Rows 16 and 18: Rep Row 10.

Row 17: HBK across.

Row 19: K2tog, work HBK until you reach last 2 sts, k2tog—26 sts.

Row 20: HBP across.

Row 21: HBK across.

Row 22: P2tog, work HBP until you reach last 2 sts, p2tog—24 sts.

Row 23: Change to smaller needles and BO in HBK. This will give you an edge that naturally folds over.

FINISHING

Place WS of bag panels together. Using a crochet hook and starting at either top edge of bag, sc around edge of bag, seaming edges together. Weave in all ends.

LINING THE TOTE (OPTIONAL)

Turn your finished tote inside out.

Fold over each short end of the lining fabric by ½"/1.3cm toward the WS and press with an iron. Fold the lining in half, RS together, with the pressed edges at the top. Sew up both sides using a ½"/1.3cm seam allowance. Note: If you don't own a sewing machine, you can sew the lining by hand.

Turn the lining right side out and slip the tote (which is wrong side out) into the lining. Attach the lining to the tote by sewing a running stitch (page 120) along the top edge. Turn tote right side out and tuck lining inside.

CREATING HANDLES

Join belts tog and thread one end under folded-over edge about 6 sts in from side edge. Loop belt around bag, threading through corresponding spots just under folded-over edge and adjust until handles are even. Join belts to make one continuous loop.

KNIT PEARL TRIO

Libby used her very own yarn to make this gorgeous necklace, bracelet, and earrings. These knitted baubles have a texture and style like no other jewelry. Once you make a few of these pearls, you'll be able to whip up an entire set in no time, making it an ideal last-minute gift.

Skill Level: Easy   Design by: Libby Summers

MATERIALS AND TOOLS

- Libby Summers Chunky (100% wool; 1.75oz/50g = 55yds/50m); (A): 1 ball, color Cream 100 (Yuraq)—approximately 55yds/50m of bulky weight yarn (5)

- Oddments of Manos del Uruguay Serena (60% alpaca, 40% cotton; 1.76oz/50g = 170yds/155m); (B): color 9095 Lily Pad—approximately 170yds/155m of sport-weight yarn

- Knitting needles: 8mm (size 11 U.S.) or size to obtain gauge

- Tapestry needle

- Two sets of magnetic clasps, one for necklace and one for bracelet

- Two stud earring backs measuring approximately 1cm in diameter

GAUGE

- 12 sts/15 rows = 4"/10cm in St st.

FINISHED MEASUREMENTS

- Necklace: 16½"/42 cm long; each pearl has a circumference of approximately 2¾"/7cm

- Bracelet: 7"/18cm long; each pearl has a circumference of approximately 2¾"/7cm

- Earrings: Each pearl has a circumference of approximately 2½"/6.5cm

instructions for necklace

Note: Make 15 pearls for a choker. If you wish to make a longer necklace, add 2 pearls for every 2 ¼"/5.5cm in additional length desired.

With A, CO 6 sts.

Work 4 rows in St st.

BO on RS kwise, leaving a 4"/10cm tail.

SEW SQUARES INTO PEARLS

Thread a tapestry needle with the BO tail and sew a running stitch all the way around the square, pulling the yarn gently as you go along, and finally gathering it up tightly in the center to form the pearl.

To give the pearl shape, sew a second gathering row of 5 evenly spaced sts a couple of sts out from the first gathering row. Pull tog into the center on top of the first row of gathered sts.

Rep these steps for all your knitted squares.

FINISHING

Cut three 25½"/65cm strands of B and thread them onto a tapestry needle.

Insert needle into one side of pearl and pull through to the other, leaving about 2"/5cm of thread poking out the end. Tie a small knot right up against the pearl. Rep until you have threaded all pearls.

**Thread the needle through one of the magnetic clasps and pull through, leaving about ¾"/2cm of thread between the clasp and the last pearl. Bring the needle over and under this ¾"/2cm in order to create a knot close to the last pearl to secure the clasp. Insert needle through the center of the knot to secure and then fasten off by inserting all the way through the pearl. Finish off in the knot between the last two pearls on the strand.

Rep from ** for the other end of the necklace, using the 2"/5cm of yarn that you left when you started threading.

Instructions for Bracelet

Work as for necklace, working 6 pearls in total and using 12"/30.5cm lengths of B for threading.

Instructions for Earrings

(Make 2)

With A, CO 4 sts.

Work 3 rows in St st.

BO on WS pwise, leaving a 4"/10cm tail.

FINISHING

With WS of knitted square facing you, place stud earring back in center of square with spike pointing upwards.

Thread a tapestry needle with the BO yarn tail and sew a running stitch all the way round the square, pulling the yarn gently as you go along. Gather it up tightly in the center underneath the butterfly of the earring back. Secure and weave in ends.

ARROWHEAD LACE SCARF

The chevron lace of this soft scarf gives it a light, airy feel, though its super bulky yarn will keep you happily bundled if the temperature dips. Finish each edge with a pretty single-crochet scallop that also stops the edges from curling in.

Skill Level: Intermediate   Design by: Caroline Brooke

MATERIALS AND TOOLS

◆ DROPS Garn Studio Eskimo Mix (100% wool; 1.8oz/50g = 55yds/50m); 4 skeins, color Medium Blue/Purple #41—approximately 220yd/200m of super bulky weight yarn (6)

◆ Knitting needles: 9mm (size 13 U.S.) or size to obtain gauge

◆ Crochet hook: 8mm (size L-11 U.S.)

◆ Tapestry Needle

GAUGE

◆ 12sts/14 rows = 4"/10cm in St st

SPECIAL ABBREVIATION

◆ sl2tbl: Insert needle in next 2 sts as if to k2tog and sl both stitches onto right needle. K1 then sl both slipped stitches over.

FINISHED MEASUREMENTS

◆ 72" x 6" (183cm x 15cm)

instructions

CO 19 sts.

ARROWHEAD LACE PATTERN

Row 1 (RS): K1, k2tog, yo, k1, yo, k3, ssk, k1, k2tog, k3, yo, k1, yo, ssk, k1.

Row 2 and all WS rows: K1, p17, k1.

Row 3: K1, k2tog, (yo, k2) twice, ssk, k1, k2tog, (k2, yo) twice, ssk, k1.

Row 5: K1, k2tog, yo, k1, yo, k2tog, yo, k1, ssk, k1, k2tog, k1, yo, ssk, yo, k1, yo, ssk, k1.

Row 7: K1, (k2tog, yo) twice, k2, yo, ssk, k1, k2tog, yo, k2, (yo, ssk) twice, k1.

Row 9: K1, k2tog, yo, k5, yo, sl2tbl, yo, k5, yo, ssk, k1.

Row 11: K1, k2tog, yo, k13, yo, ssk, k1.

Row 13: K3, yo, k4, ssk, k1, k2tog, k4, yo, k3.

Row 14: K1, p17, k1.

Rep these rows 15 times.

Rep Rows 1–5 once.

BO on WS.

Do not break off yarn.

FINISHING

With crochet hook, work 1 row sc around all four edges of the scarf, beginning on one long edge and ending on the BO edge. When you reach the starting point, turn and work as follows:

Ch 8, work 1 sc into the 5th stitch of the BO edge. Rep three times to reach the end of the BO row, forming 4 scallops.

Turn and work 8 sc into each of the scallops and 1 sc into each sc of the previous row. When you reach the end, work 1 sc into last st, break yarn, and weave in all ends.

Rep this along the CO edge of the scarf. Block (page 120).

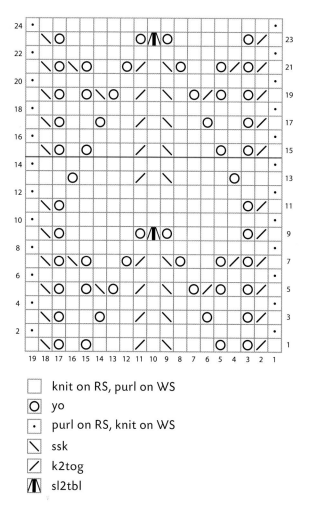

	knit on RS, purl on WS
O	yo
•	purl on RS, knit on WS
\	ssk
/	k2tog
/\	sl2tbl

BRAIDED CABLE PILLOW

This pillow covers the home décor bases—it is comfy *and* stylish. Its luxurious texture and snooze-here softness will dress up any sofa, but don't worry if it sees a spill or two. It's removable (thanks, zipper!) and knit with washable acrylic yarn, which makes it safe for important activities like late-night chocolate snacking.

Skill Level: Intermediate   Design by: Erin Black

MATERIALS AND TOOLS

- Bernat Chunky Big Ball (100% acrylic; 14.11oz/400g = 431yds/394m) 2 skeins, color Aran—approximately 862yds/788m of super bulky weight yarn (6)

- Knitting needles: 12mm (size 17 U.S.) circular needle, 29"/74cm long or size to obtain gauge

- Cable needle

- Tapestry needle

- 20"/51cm zipper

- 26"/66cm square pillow form

GAUGE

- 7 sts/10 rows = 4"/10cm in St st with two strands held tog

SPECIAL ABBREVIATIONS

- C6F: Slip 3 stitches purlwise to cable needle, hold to front of work. Knit 3 sts from left needle, knit 3 sts from cable needle.

- C6B: Slip 3 stitches purlwise to cable needle, hold to back of work. Knit 3 sts from left needle, knit 3 sts from cable needle.

FINISHED MEASUREMENTS

- 25"/64cm square

instructions

Note: Can't find the Bernat Chunky Big Ball? Look for the Bernat Softee Chunky yarn in Natural #28008 or Linen #28021 in an equivalent yardage.

Using two strands of yarn held tog, CO 40 sts.

Row 1: K17, p2, k15, p2, k4.

Row 2 and all even rows: P4, k2, p15, k2, p17.

Row 3: K17, p2, k3, (C6F) twice, p2, k4.

Row 5: Rep Row 1.

Row 7: K17, p2, (C6B) twice, k3, p2, k4.

Row 8: Rep row 2.

Rep Rows 1–8 seventeen more times. BO.

FINISHING

Fold the pillow cover in half, aligning the CO and BO edges. Seam the two side seams together using mattress stitch (page 119).

Seam together the CO and BO edges. Install the zipper in the center of the seam: Unzip the zipper. Pin into place, placing one side of the

zipper tape facedown onto the right side of the pillow cover seam. Pin the zipper teeth close to the knitting, but not so close that the stitches might get caught in the zipper. With a needle and yarn, sew the zipper into place using a backstitch.

Repeat these steps for the opposite side of the pillow, matching the right side of the zipper to the right side of the knitting. Sew across the coils at each zipper end, securing in place.

Stuff the cover with your pillow form.

CRESCENT SHAWL

CRESCENT SHAWL

This crescent-shaped shawl is worked from the bottom up with wrapless short rows. Wear it on those days when you need just a little extra warmth around your shoulders, or don it with a pretty party dress and add some colorful texture to an elegant night on the town.

Skill Level: Intermediate   Design by: Meghan Jones

MATERIALS AND TOOLS
- Knitpicks Wool of the Andes Bulky (100% wool; 3.5oz/100g = 137yds/125m); 2 skeins, color Beach Glass #25554—approximately 274yds/250.5m of bulky weight yarn ⑤

- Knitting needles: 6mm (size 10 U.S.) circular needles, 29"/74cm long or size to obtain gauge

- Stitch markers

- Tapestry needle

GAUGE
- 9 sts/13 rows = 4"/10cm in pattern after blocking

FINISHED MEASUREMENTS
- 69"/175cm wide and 18"/46cm tall after blocking

instructions

Using Knitted-On Method (page 113), CO 137 sts.

BORDER
Row 1: K2, pm, *work stitches 1–12 of chart; rep from * 10 times more, work stitch 13 of chart, (2 sts remain), pm, k2.

Rows 2–12: Rep Row 1, slipping markers and working Rows 2–12 of chart.

MAIN BODY
SHORT ROWS
Note: Turn, but do not wrap at the end of each short row.

Row 1 (RS): K67, yo, sk2p, yo, k3, turn.

Row 2: P9, turn.

Row 3: *Yo, sk2p, yo, k3; rep from * once more, turn.

Row 4: P15, turn.

Row 5: *Yo, sk2p, yo, k3; rep from * twice more, turn.

Row 6: P to gap, p3.

Rep Rows 5 and 6 nineteen times, working an additional rep of (yo, sk2p, yo, k3) every RS row—2 sts remain unworked before markers.

FULL ROWS

Row 1 (RS): K to marker, sm, p1, k1, *k3, yo, sk2p, yo; rep from * to 5 sts before last marker, k3, k1, p1, sm, k to end.

Row 2 (WS): K2, sm, p to marker, sm, k2.

Row 3: K2, sm, p1, k1, *yo, sk2p, yo, k3; rep from * to 5 sts before last marker, yo, sk2p, yo, p1, k1, sm, k2.

Row 4: Knit.

BO: K1, *pass the knitted st back to left needle, k2tog tbl; rep from * for rem sts.

FINISHING

Weave in all ends. Using blocking wires and pins, wet-block shawl to dimensions specified in measurements.

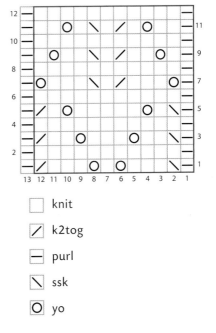

	knit
╱	k2tog
─	purl
╲	ssk
O	yo

TWO-TONE CLUTCH

Give yourself an excuse to show off your knitting everywhere you go by adding this little clutch to your rotation of accessories. Knit it up in your favorite chunky cotton for a more summer-friendly vibe, play with glittery yarn for an evening statement piece, or, for extra school spirit, use it to sport your team's colors.

Skill Level: Easy   Design by: Meredith Crawford

MATERIALS AND TOOLS

- Plymouth baby alpaca Grande (100% baby alpaca; 3.5oz/100g = 110yds/101m); (A), 1 skein color Coral #6010; (B), 1 skein color Fawn #0202—approximately 220yds/201m of super bulky weight yarn (6)

- Knitting needles: 6.5mm (size 10½ U.S.) or size to obtain gauge

- Tapestry needle

- 1 button, 1"/2.5cm in diameter

- 11" wide x 7½" tall (28cm x 19cm) piece of fabric for lining

- Iron

- Sewing machine or needle and thread

GAUGE

- 12 sts/18 rows = 4"/10cm in St st

FINISHED MEASUREMENTS

- Folded: 6.5"/16.5cm tall

- Open: 11" tall x 10" wide (28cm x 25cm)

instructions

CLUTCH FRONT

With A, CO 32 sts.

Rows 1–12: Work in St st.

Row 13–29: Change to B and cont in St st. BO.

CLUTCH BACK AND FLAP

With A, CO 32 sts.

Rows 1–12: Work in St st.

Rows 13–29: Change to B and cont in St st, ending with a k row.

Row 30: K the first 3 sts, p to the last 3 sts, k3.

Row 31: Knit.

Rep Rows 30 and 31 four times, then rep Row 30 once more.

Next (buttonhole) row: K15, BO 2 sts for the buttonhole, k15.

Next (buttonhole) row: K3, p until you reach the buttonhole, turn your work and CO 2 sts, turn your work back around and p to the last 3 sts, k3.

Rep Rows 30 and 31, then rep Row 30 once more.

Work 3 rows in Garter St.

BO.

FINISHING

Use mattress stitch (page 119) to join the sides and bottom of the clutch.

Line the button up with the buttonhole and sew it to the clutch front.

LINING THE BAG

Turn your finished clutch inside out.

Fold over each short end of the lining fabric by ½"/1.3cm toward the WS and press with an iron.

Fold the lining in half, RS together, with the pressed edges at the top. Sew up both sides using a ½"/1.3cm seam allowance. Note: If you don't own a sewing machine, you can sew the lining by hand.

Turn the lining right side out and slip the clutch (which is wrong out) into the lining. Attach the lining to the clutch by sewing a running stitch (page 120) along the top edge.

CABLE POUF OTTOMAN

This pouf adds extra seating—and knitting!—to your home décor. It's cleverly stuffed with a bundled comforter and cinched closed with a drawstring, making it easy to clean. If you don't have a comforter to fill it with, any blanket, pillow(s), or beanbag will do. Just make sure you find one in a color that complements your yarn, so it blends in nicely behind your stitches.

MATERIALS AND TOOLS

- Bernat Chunky Big Ball (100% acrylic; 14.11oz/400g = 431yds/394m); 2 skeins, color Granite—approximately 862yds/788m of super bulky weight yarn (6)

- Knitting needles: 12 mm (size 17 U.S.) circular needle, 29"/74cm long or size to obtain gauge

- Cable needle

- Tapestry needle

- 22mm cord lock toggle

- Queen size comforter for stuffing

GAUGE

- 7 sts/10 rows = 4"/10cm in St st with two strands held tog

SPECIAL ABBREVIATION

- C6F: Slip 3 stitches purlwise to cable needle, hold to front of work. Knit 3 stitches from left needle, knit 3 stitches from cable needle.

FINISHED MEASUREMENTS

- 15" diameter x 18" high (38cm x 46cm)

instructions

Note: Can't find the Bernat Chunky Big Ball? Look for the Bernat Softee Chunky yarn in Grey Heather #28046 or True Grey #28044.

Using two strands of yarn held tog, CO 48 sts.

Rows 1, 3, and 5: K11, p2, k6, p2, k6, p2, k6, p2, k11.

Row 2 and all even rows: P11, k2, p6, k2, p6, k2, p6, k2, p11.

Row 7: K11, p2, (C6F, p2) three times, k11.

Row 8: Rep Row 2.

Rep Rows 1–8 eleven more times.

FINISHING

BO loosely, leaving a 108"/274cm tail. Align the cast-on and bind-off edges and seam them together with the tail using mattress stitch (page 119) to form a tube.

Cut one double strand of yarn 60"/152cm long and weave it into each stitch along one open edge of the seamed tube. Pull the yarn taut to cinch the top of the tube and close the opening. Tie off the yarn and weave in the loose ends.

Cut a double strand of yarn 72"/183cm long and weave into each stitch along the remaining open edge of the tube. Secure the two yarn ends together with the toggle.

Fold the comforter length-wise into thirds and roll the comforter, starting at the short edge, into a cylinder. Place the rolled up comforter into the pouf, cinch the cover tightly, and secure with the toggle. Stuff the yarn ends into the pouf. Flip the pouf toggle side down to display.

GOTHIC LACE WRAP

The gorgeous lace in this pattern was inspired by stained glass windows in European medieval Gothic churches. Finish it with a chevron lace edge that creates a hem you'll be dying to show off.

Skill Level: Intermediate   Design by: Caroline Brooke

MATERIALS AND TOOLS

- DROPS Garn Studio Eskimo Yarn (100% wool; 1.8oz/50g = 55yds/50m); 8 skeins, color Light Gray Green #55— approximately 440yds/400m of super bulky weight yarn (6)
- Knitting needles: 9mm knitting needles (size 13 U.S.) or size to obtain gauge
- Crochet hook: 8mm (size L-11 U.S.)
- Tapestry Needle

GAUGE

- 12sts/14 rows = 4"/10cm in St st.

FINISHED MEASUREMENTS

- 71" x 15½" (180cm x 39cm)

instructions

CO 47 sts.

Row 1 (RS): K3, ssk, k3, yo, k1, yo, (k3, sl1, k2tog, psso, k3, yo, k1, yo) three times, k3, k2tog, k3.

Row 2 and every WS row: K2, p43, k2.

Repeat these 2 rows twelve times.

Row 27: K3, ssk, k2, yo, k3, yo, (k2, sl1, k2tog, psso, k2, yo, k3, yo) three times, k2, k2tog, k3.

Row 29: K3, ssk, k1, yo, k5, yo, (k1, sl1, K2tog, psso, k1, yo, k5, yo) three times, k1, k2tog, k3.

Row 31: K3, ssk, yo, k7, yo, (sl1, k2tog, psso, yo, k7, yo) three times, k2tog, k3.

Row 32: K2, p to last 2 sts, k2.

Row 33–40: Rep Rows 31 and 32 four times.

Row 41: K5, yo, ssk, k3, k2tog, (yo, k3, yo, ssk, k3, k2tog) three times, yo, k5.

Row 43: K6, yo, ssk, k1, k2tog, (yo, k5, yo, ssk, k1, k2tog) three times, yo, k6.

Row 45: K7, yo, sl1, k2tog, psso, yo, k7, (yo, sl1, k2tog, psso, yo, k7) three times.

Row 47: K5, k2tog, yo, k3, (yo, ssk, k3, k2tog, yo, k3) three times, yo, ssk, k5.

Row 49: K4, k2tog, yo, k5, (yo, ssk, k1, k2tog, yo, k5) three times, yo, ssk, k4.

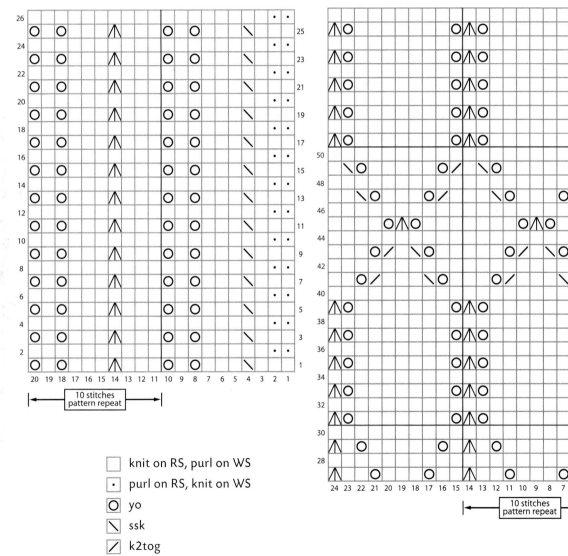

10 stitches
pattern repeat

☐ knit on RS, purl on WS

• purl on RS, knit on WS

Ⓞ yo

◺ ssk

◹ k2tog

◮ slip 1, k2tog, pass slip st over

10 stitches
pattern repeat

Row 50: K2, p to last 2 sts, k2.

Rep Rows 31–50 five times.

Rep Rows 31 and 32 four times.

Rep Rows 41– 45.

Rep Row 50.

Rep Rows 1 and 2 thirteen times.

BO on the last WS row. Do not break yarn.

FINISHING

With crochet hook and RS facing, work along BO edge as follows:

Work 1 sc into each of the first 8 BO sts. This will take you to the point of the first chevron. Ch3, then work 1 sc into the same st. *Skip the next st, then work 1 sc into each of the next 8 BO stitches, work 1 sc into next st, ch3, then work 1 sc into the same st. Rep from * twice. Skip the next st and work 1 sc into next 7 sts. Break yarn and thread through rem st.

Join yarn to crochet hook and following the same procedure, work 1 row of sc along the CO edge of the shawl, taking care to work 1 sc, 3 ch, and 1 sc into each of the stitches at the chevron points, as on the BO end. Note that there are 5 chevron points on the CO edge as opposed to 4 on the BO edge, and that they are in a different position.

Weave in all ends.

TECH CASE

There's no better way to keep your tech devices safe than with a chunky knit case. This pattern is written for a small e-reader, but you'll find instructions on how to easily adapt it to fit other devices.

Skill Level: Intermediate   Design by: Nguyen Le

MATERIALS AND TOOLS

- Cascade 128 Superwash (100% Superwash Merino Wool; 3.5oz/100g = 128yds/117m); 1 skein, color Silver #1946—approximately 128yds/117m of bulky weight yarn **⑤**

- Knitting needles: 6mm (size 10 U.S.) or size to obtain gauge

- Crochet hook: 5mm (size H-8 U.S.)

- Cable needle

- Tapestry needle

- Large button

- Optional fabric for lining: 6½" (16.5cm) x 14¼" (36cm)

GAUGE

- 18 sts/24 rows = 4"/10cm over cable pattern

SPECIAL ABBREVIATION

- CB8: Sl 4 sts to cn and hold in back, k4 sts, k4 sts from cn.

FINISHED MEASUREMENTS

- 5¼" x 7" (13cm x 18cm) stretched

instructions

CO 24 sts.

Rows 1–5: Work in k1, p1 ribbing.

Rows 6, 8, 10, and 12 (WS): (P1, k1) twice, k4, p8, k4, (p1, k1) twice.

Rows 7, 9, and 11 (RS): (K1, p1) twice, p4, k8, p4, (k1, p1) twice.

Row 13 (cable row): (K1, p1) twice, p4, CB8, p4, (k1, p1) twice.

Rep rows 6–13 eight more times, then rows 6–12 once.

Work in seed st for 5 rows.

BO in seed st and leave a long tail for seaming one side.

FINISHING

Block finished piece (page 120) to 5" x 15" (12.5cm x 38cm), and fold in half lengthwise. With tapestry needle, use a mattress stitch (page 119) to sew the sides together. Weave in ends.

With crochet hook, attach yarn to the top center of the back edge of the case and ch20. Use a tapestry needle to sew the end to the beginning of the ch, making the button loop. Sew a button to the top center of the front of the case and weave in ends.

OPTIONAL FABRIC LINING

Note: If you don't own a sewing machine, you can sew the lining by hand.

Cut fabric to a 6½" x 14¼" (16.5cm x 36cm) piece and fold it in half lengthwise. The fold is the bottom edge, and the open 6½"/16.5cm edge is the top.

Fold the top edges down ½"/1.3cm to the WS and press with an iron. Pin the side edges RS together and sew with a ½"/1.3cm seam allowance along each side.

Insert the sewn lining into the knit case WS together and pin along the top edge. Whipstitch (page 120) along the edge with matching thread and secure.

ADAPTING THE PATTERN TO FIT OTHER DEVICES

This cable knit tech case can be easily adapted to fit your specific device. There are a couple ways to do this:

• Multiply the number of sts (4.5) and rows (6) per inch by the width and height of your device. This will give you the CO number and number of rows needed. Be sure to include ¾–1" (1.9–2.5cm) to the number of rows for the bottom edge of the device and an extra row on either side for sewing up.

• If the height isn't tall enough to add another whole 8 row cable repeat, you can simply add extra rows to both top seed st borders. If you need to add more CO sts to the width, you can widen the seed st side borders.

• If you're adapting this case for a much larger or smaller case, such as an e-reader, laptop, or cell phone, you can add more stitches evenly to each section (seed st borders, purl borders on either side of the cable, and 8 st back cable).

• If you're adding stitches to the center cable, you'll want to make the cable rows further apart and on an even row, so they don't twist up too tightly. The same applies if you are removing stitches from the center cable; make the cable rows closer together to keep an even twist of the cable on an even-numbered row.

Note: The knit case will be stretchy and forgiving of the exact size of your device, but you'll need to make the lining with a little extra room.

COZY CABLE HAT

Texture and cables define this cozy, classic unisex hat. Skip the pompom if you want to give the hat a more streamlined look or try it in a soft, heathery charcoal for a darker look. See page 60 for the matching Cozy Cable Mittens.

Skill Level: Intermediate   Design by: Vanessa Ewing

MATERIALS AND TOOLS

- Plymouth Baby Alpaca Grande (100% baby alpaca; 3.5oz/100g = 110yds/101m); 2 skeins, color Aran #8542— approximately 220yds/201m of bulky weight yarn (5)
- Knitting needles: 5.5mm (size 9 U.S.) circular needle, 16"/41cm long
- 6.5mm (size 10½ U.S.) circular needle, 16"/41cm long and double pointed needles or size to obtain gauge
- Stitch marker
- Cable needle
- Piece of cardboard or a book that is 5"/13cm wide for pom-pom (optional)

GAUGE

- 16 sts/22 rows = 4"/10cm in Cable Pattern with larger needles
- 4 sts/4 rows = 1"/2.5cm in k2, p2 ribbing with smaller needles, slightly stretched

SPECIAL ABBREVIATIONS

- C4B: sl 2 sts to cable needle and hold to back, k2, k2 from cable needle
- C4F: sl 2 sts to cable needle and hold to front, k2, k2 from cable needle

FINISHED MEASUREMENTS

- 21 (24)"/53 (61)cm circumference to fit adult sizes small/medium and large (shown in small/medium)

CABLE PATTERN

- Worked in the rnd overmultiple of 12 sts
  Rnd 1: *K2, p2, k2, C4B, p2; rep from * around.
  Rnd 2: *K2, p2, k6, p2; rep from * around.
  Rnd 3: *K2, p2, C4F, k2, p2; rep from * around.
  Rnd 4: *P4, k6, p2; rep from * around.
  Rep these 4 rnds for pattern st.

instructions

Note: Pattern is written for smallest size, with larger size in parenthesis. If only one number is given, it applies to both sizes.

With smaller circular needle, CO 84 (96) sts. Pm and join in the rnd, being careful not to twist sts.

Work in K2, p2 ribbing for 8 rnds.

Switch to larger circular needle and begin working in cable pattern, following either the written or the charted instructions. If working the charted instructions, work all rnds from right to left.

Work 7 (8) full repeats of the cable pattern—28 (32) rnds.

SHAPE CROWN

Rnd 1 (dec): *K2, p2, k2, sl 2 sts to cable needle and hold to back, k2tog, k2tog from cable needle, p2; rep from * around—70 (80) sts.

Rnd 2: *K2, p2, k4, p2; rep from * around.

Rnd 3 (dec): *K2, p2, sl 2 sts to cable needle and hold to front, k2tog, k2tog from cable needle, p2; rep from * around—56 (64) sts.

Rnd 4: *P4, k2, p2; rep from * around.

Rnd 5 (dec): *K2, p2tog, sl 1 st to cable needle and hold to front, k1, k1 from cable needle, p2tog, k2; rep from * around—42 (48) sts.

Switch to larger dpns.

COZY CABLE HAT

Rnd 6 (dec): *K1, k2tog; rep from * around—28 (32) sts.

Rnd 7 (dec): *K2tog; rep from * around—14 (16) sts.

Rnd 8 (dec): *K2tog; rep from * around—7 (8) sts.

FINISHING

Break yarn and draw through rem sts. Weave in all ends.

POMPOM (OPTIONAL)

With rem yarn, make a 3"/8cm diameter pompom by wrapping yarn around the piece of cardboard or book. Carefully remove the wrapped yarn and tie a 10"/25cm piece of yarn tightly in the center of these strands. Cut the loops at both ends. Trim the strands to shape into a ball, but leave the two long pieces un-cut. Once pompom is shaped, use two long pieces to attach it to the top of the hat.

CABLE PATTERN

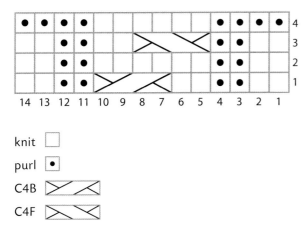

knit ▯
purl ▪
C4B
C4F

COZY CABLE MITTENS

These cozy mittens are knit in the round—woohoo!—eliminating the need for seaming. You'll memorize the stitch pattern in no time, making it the perfect project for the weekend or for taking to your stitch group. See page 56 for the matching Cozy Cable Hat.

Skill Level: Intermediate   Design by: Vanessa Ewing

MATERIALS AND TOOLS
- Plymouth Baby Alpaca Grande (100% baby alpaca; 3.5oz/100g = 110yds/101m); 1 skein, color Aran #8542—approximately 110yds/101m of bulky weight yarn (5)
- Knitting needles: 5.5mm (size 9 U.S.) and 6.5mm (size 10½ U.S.) double pointed needles, 16"/41cm long or size to obtain gauge
- Stitch marker
- Cable needle
- Scrap yarn

GAUGE
- 16 sts/22 rows = 4"/10cm in cable pattern with larger needles
- 4 sts/4 rows = 1"/2.5cm in k2, p2 ribbing with smaller needles, slightly stretched

SPECIAL ABBREVIATION
- C4B: Sl 2 sts to cable needle and hold to back, k2, k2 from cable needle
- C4F: Sl 2 sts to cable needle and hold to front, k2, k2 from cable needle
- kf&b: Knit into the front and back of the same stitch

FINISHED MEASUREMENTS
- 7"/18cm circumference to fit average woman's hand

CABLE PATTERN
- Worked in the rnd over 14 sts
  Rnd 1: K2, p2, k2, C4B, p2, k2.
  Rnd 2: K2, p2, k6, p2, k2.
  Rnd 3: K2, p2, C4F, k2, p2, k2.
  Rnd 4: P4, k6, p4.
  Rep these 4 rnds for pattern st.

instructions

RIGHT MITTEN

With smaller dpns, CO 28 sts. Divide sts evenly onto 3 dpns. Pm and join in the round, being careful not to twist sts.

Work in K2, p2 ribbing for 10 rnds.

Change to larger dpns.

Pattern Setup: Work 14 sts in cable pattern rnd 1, pm, k14.

Next Rnd: Work in cable pattern rnd 2 to marker, sl marker, k to end of round.**

SHAPE THUMB

Rnd 1 (inc): Work cable pattern rnd 3 to marker, sl marker, [kf&b] twice, k to end of rnd—30 sts.

Rnd 2 and all even rnds: Work next rnd of cable pattern to marker, sl marker, k to end of rnd.

Rnd 3 (inc): Work cable pattern rnd 1 to marker, sl marker, kf&b, k2, kf&b, k to end of rnd—32 sts.

Rnd 5 (inc): Work cable pattern rnd 3 to marker, sl marker, kf&b, k4, kf&b, k to end of rnd—34 sts.

Rnd 7 (inc): Work cable pattern rnd 1 to marker, sl marker, kf&b, k6, kf&b, k to end of rnd—36 sts.

Rnd 9 (inc): Work cable pattern rnd 3 to marker, sl marker, kf&b, k8, kf&b, k to end of rnd—38 sts.

DIVIDE THUMB

Next rnd: Work cable pattern rnd 4 to marker, remove marker, place the next 12 sts onto scrap yarn, CO 2 sts onto the right hand needle using the backward loop method, k to end of rnd—28 sts on the needle and 12 sts on the scrap yarn. ***

Next rnd: Work next rnd of cable pattern across 14 sts, k to end of rnd.

Rep this rnd for 16 more times, continuing in cable pattern and ending after having worked rnd 1 of cable pattern.

SHAPE TOP

Rnd 1 (dec): Ssk, p2, k6, p2, k2tog, ssk, k to last 2 sts, k2tog—24 sts.

Rnd 2: K1, p2, C4F, k2, p2, k1, k to end of round.

Rnd 3 (dec): Ssk, p1, k6, p1, k2tog, ssk, k to last 2 sts, k2tog—20 sts.

Rnd 4: K1, p1, k2, C4B, p1, k to end of round.

Rnd 5 (dec): *Ssk, k6, k2tog; rep from * once more—16 sts.

Rnd 6: K1, C4F, k to end of rnd.

Rnd 7 (dec): *Ssk, k4, k2tog; rep from * once more—12 sts.

Work the rem sts in Kitchener st (page 119). Cut yarn and weave in all ends.

LEFT MITTEN

Work same as Right Mitten to **.

SHAPE THUMB

Rnd 1 (inc): Work in cable pattern rnd 3 to marker, sl marker, k12, (kf&b) twice—30 sts.

Rnd 2 and all even rows: Work next round of cable pattern to marker, sl marker, k to end of round.

Rnd 3 (inc): Work in cable pattern rnd 1 to marker, sl marker, k12 kf&b, k2, kf&b—32 sts.

Rnd 5 (inc): Work in cable pattern rnd 3 to marker, sl marker, k12, kf&b, k4, kf&b—34 sts.

Rnd 7 (inc): Work in cable pattern rnd 1 to marker, sl marker, k12, kf&b, k6, kf&b—36 sts.

Rnd 9 (inc): Work in cable pattern rnd 3 to marker, sl marker, k12, kf&b, k8, kf&b—38 sts.

DIVIDE THUMB

Next rnd: Work in cable pattern rnd 4 to marker, remove marker, k12, place the next 12 sts onto scrap yarn, CO 2 sts onto the right hand needle using the backward loop method—28 sts on the needle and 12 sts on the scrap yarn.

Work same as right mitten thumb from ***.

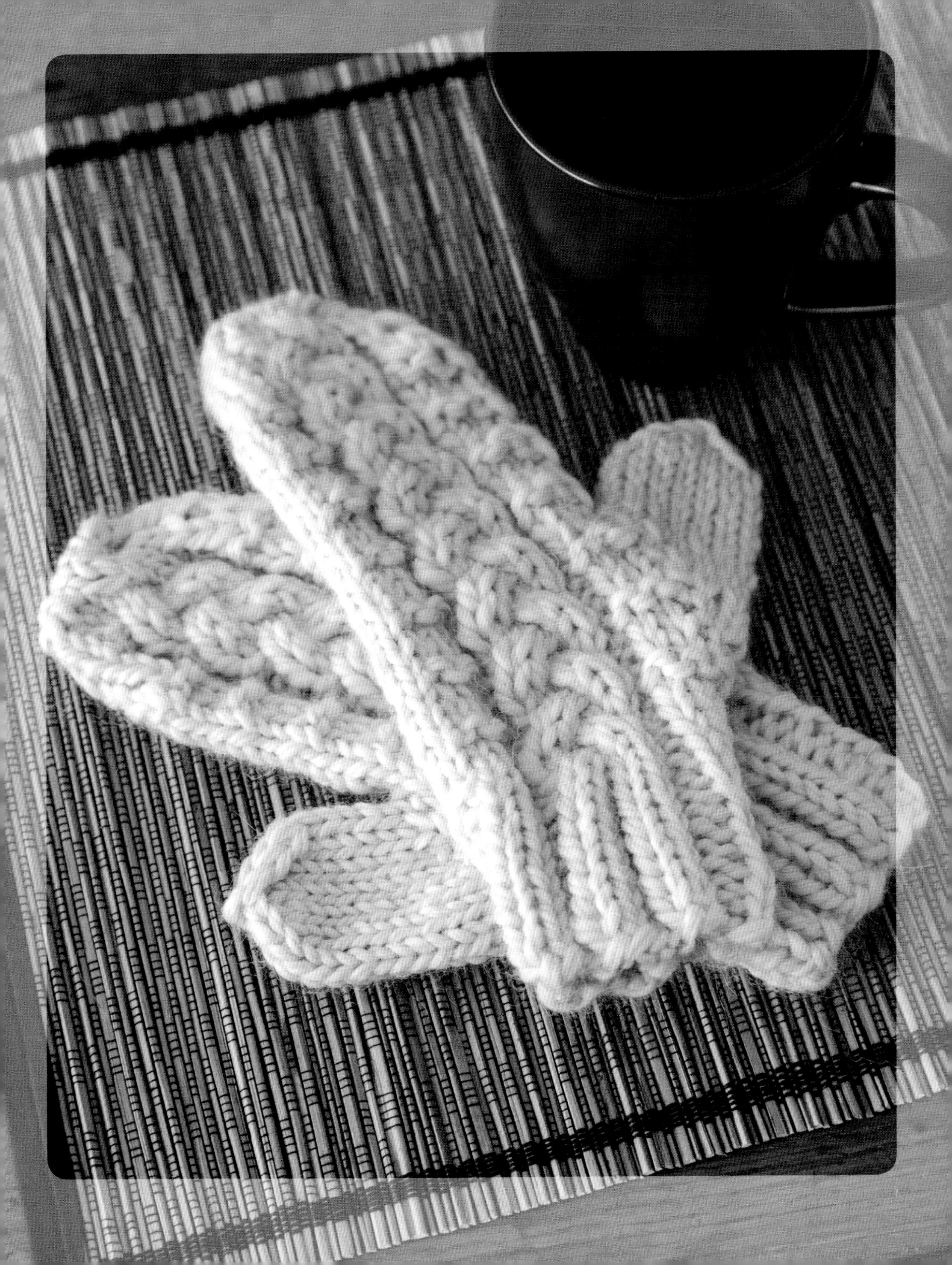

THUMB (FOR BOTH LEFT AND RIGHT MITTEN)

With RS facing, sl the 12 sts from the thumb onto 3 dpns.

Join yarn and k across sts. Pick up and k 2 sts from the CO of the mitten palm—14 sts.

Cont to work in St st for 7 more rnds.

Shape Top of Thumb

Rnd 1 (dec): *Ssk, k3, k2tog; rep from * once more—10 sts.

Rnd 2 (dec): *Ssk, k1, k2tog; rep from * once more—6 sts.

Rnd 3 (dec): *Sl1, k2tog, psso; rep from * once more—2 sts.

FINISHING

Cut yarn and draw through rem sts. Weave in all ends.

CABLE PATTERN

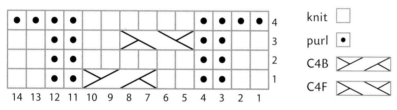

knit	☐	
purl	⊡	
C4B	⧓	
C4F	⧓	

LACE
VEST

LACE VEST

Three strategically placed buttons and an airy lace pattern let you button this top anywhere you'd like to create several different looks. Button at the sides of the hips in the ribbing area for a more traditional wrap, or take the corners up near the shoulders for a bolero fit with a draped cowl neckline. Wear the top diagonally with one button on the hip and one near the shoulder, or even turn it around backwards.

Skill Level: Intermediate   Design by: Joleen Kraft

MATERIALS AND TOOLS
- Bernat Alpaca (70% acrylic, 30% alpaca; 3.5oz/100g = 120yds/110m); 2 (3, 3) skeins, color Tomato #93531—approximately 240 (360, 360)yds/219.5 (329, 329)m of bulky weight yarn (5)
- Knitting needles: 8mm (size 11 U.S.)
- Three buttons (two matching and one hidden)

GAUGE
- 12 sts/16 rows = 4"/10cm in lace pattern repeat.

SPECIAL ABBREVIATION
- dr: drop

FINISHED MEASUREMENTS
- 18 (20, 22)"/46 (51, 56)cm length from top to bottom with positive ease

instructions

Note: Slip the first st of every row to create a selvage.

BACK

CO 38 (42, 46) sts.

Row 1: *K3 (4, 4), p3 (4, 4); rep from* to last st, k1.

Row 2: *P3 (4, 4), k3 (4, 4); rep from * to last st, p1.

Rows 3–6: Rep rows 1 & 2.

Row 7: Knit.

Row 8 (Begin Lace Pattern): *P4, yo; rep from * to last st, p1.

Row 9: *Yo, dr1, sl1st, k3, psso 3 k sts; rep from * to last st, k1.

Row 10: *P2tog, yo, p2; rep from * to last st, p1.

Row 11: Knit.

Row 12: P2 *p4, yo; rep from * to last 3 sts, p3.

Row 13: K2, *yo, dr1, sl1, k3, psso 3 k sts; rep from * to last 3 sts, k3.

Row 14: P2, *p2tog, yo, p2; rep from * to last 3 sts, p3.

Row 15: Knit.

Rep rows 8–15 a total of 7 (8, 9) times. BO on last k row.

LEFT FRONT

CO 38 (42, 46).

Rep rows 1–6 of Back.

Row 7: K to last 5 sts, (k2tog) twice, k1.

Row 8: P2, *p4, yo; rep from * to last st, p1.

Row 9: *Yo, dr1, sl1st, k3, psso 3 k sts; rep from * to last 3 sts, yo, k2tog, k1.

Row 10: P2, *p2tog, yo, p2; rep from * to last st, p1.

Row 11: Rep Row 7.

Row 12: P2, *p4, yo; rep from * to last 3 sts, p3.

Row 13: K2, *yo, dr1, sl1, k3, psso 3 k sts; rep from * to last 3 sts, yo, k2tog, k1.

Row 14: P2, *p2tog, yo, p2; rep from * to last 3 sts, p2tog, yo, p1.

Row 15: Rep Row 7.

Rep rows 8–15 five more times, then rep rows 8–14.

For size small, BO.

Sizes Medium and Large Only

For medium and large sizes, repeat the following (1, 2) times:

Note: There are no decreases on knit rows.

Next row: Knit.

Next row: *P4, yo; rep from * to last st, p1.

Next row: *Yo, dr1, sl1st, k3, psso 3 k sts; rep from * to last st, k1.

Next row: P2, *p2tog, yo, p2; rep from * to last st, p1.

Next row: Knit.

Next row: P2, *p4, yo; rep from * to last 3 sts, p3.

Next row: K2, *yo, dr1, sl1st, k3, psso 3 k sts; rep from * to last 3 sts, yo, k2tog, k1.

Next row: P2, *p2tog, yo, p2; rep from * to last 3 sts, p2tog, yo, p1.

BO.

RIGHT FRONT

CO 38 (42, 46).

Rep rows 1–6 from back.

Row 7: (K2tog) twice, knit to end.

Row 8: *P4, yo; rep from * to last 3 sts, p3.

Row 9: Yo, k2tog, *yo, dr1, sl1st, k3, psso 3 k sts; rep from * to last st, k1.

Row 10: *P2tog, yo, p2; rep from * to last 3 sts, p3.

Row 11: Rep Row 7.

Row 12: P2, *p4, yo; rep from * to last 3 sts p3.

Row 13: Yo, k2tog, *yo, dr1, sl1st, k3, psso 3 k sts; rep from * to last 3 sts, k3.

Row 14: P2, *p2tog, yo, p2; rep from * to last 3 sts, p3.

Row 15: Rep Row 7.

Rep Rows 8–15 six more times, then rep Rows 8–10.

For size small, BO.

Sizes Medium and Large Only

For medium and large sizes, repeat the following (1, 2) times:

Note: there are no decreases on knit rows during this rep.

Next row: Knit.

Next row: *P4, yo; rep from * to last st, p1.

Next row: *Yo, dr1, sl1, k3, psso 3 k sts; rep from * to last st, k1.

Next row: *P4, yo; rep from * to last 3 sts, p3.

Next row: Knit.

Next row: P2, *p4, yo; rep from * to last 3 sts, p3.

Next row: Yo, k2tog, *yo, dr1, sl1, k3, psso 3 k sts; rep from * to last 3 sts, k2tog, k1.

Next row: *P4, yo; rep from * to last st, p1.
BO.

FINISHING

With WS together, stitch top shoulder edge together. To stitch side seam, skip 8 (10, 12) selvage stitches for armhole, and then continue stitching remaining selvage edges to bottom. Rep for other side. Weave in ends.

Attach matching buttons at bottom corner point of each front section. Attach the remaining button behind either of the matching buttons.

LACE LAMPSHADE
COZY

This lampshade cover is knit in the round with no seams, so your lampshade looks beautiful from any angle. It's designed to fit the most basic drum-shaped shade, and you can size it to fit both small and medium sizes. So turn on your lamp, pour some tea, and admire how the light illuminates the lace pattern.

Skill Level: Intermediate   Design by: Julie Finocchiaro

MATERIALS AND TOOLS

* Lion Brand Wool Ease Chunky (80% acrylic, 20% wool; 5oz/140g = 153yds/140m); 1 (2) skeins, Willow #630-173—approximately 153yds/140m (306yds/280m) of bulky weight yarn (5) * second shade shown in Spice #630-133

* Knitting needles: 6.5mm (size 10½ U.S.) circular needle, 16"/41cm (24"/61cm) long or size to obtain gauge

* Stitch marker

* Drum-shaped lampshade

   * Small shade: 26"/66cm top circumference, 32"/81cm bottom circumference, 7"/18cm high.

   * Medium shade: 35"/89cm top circumference, 41"/104cm bottom circumference, 9"/23cm high.

* Tapestry needle

GAUGE

* 6 sts/16 rows = 2¼" wide x 3½" long (6cm x 9cm), one repeat of the pattern

* Note: There is some stretch to the knitted cover so that it doesn't fit too loosely over the shade.

SPECIAL ABBREVIATION

* SK2togP = Sl next st to right needle kwise, knit the next 2 sts tog, pass slipped st over sts just knit

FINISHED MEASUREMENTS

* Small cozy: 24"/61cm circumference, 8"/20cm tall

* Medium cozy: 34"/86cm circumference, 10"/25cm tall

instructions

Note: As you work the cover, you can check the length by slipping half of the live stitches onto another circular needle and trying the cover on your lampshade. To keep the stitch pattern even, end on Row 16 or Row 8.

CO 78 (102) sts using the long-tail method (see page 113).

Pm and join to work in the rnd, being careful not to twist sts.

BEGIN LACE PATTERN

Rows 1, 3, 5 and 7: *Yo, SK2togP, yo, K3; rep from * to end of rnd.

Row 2 and all even rows: Knit.

Rows 9, 11, 13 and 15: *K3, yo, SK2togP, yo; rep from * to end of rnd.

Row 16: Knit.

Repeat rows 1–16 once more, then rows 1–8 zero (one) time(s).

Next 3 rows: Purl.

BO purlwise.

Note: If you find that you need extra length to fit your lampshade, add extra purl rows before binding off.

FINISHING

Weave yarn ends into back of shade cover.

FITTING THE COVER ON THE LAMPSHADE

Place the cover over the top of the lampshade with the bound-off edge at the top and gently pull down to the bottom of the shade. The top and bottom edges of the cover should roll slightly over the top and bottom of the lampshade. Smooth out the cover so the stitch pattern is evenly placed along the shade.

ADJUSTING THE SIZE OF THE COZY

If you would like to use a shade that is a different size than the ones shown in the pattern, you can adjust the size of your cover. Here's how:

Measure around the middle of the lampshade to find the circumference. To calculate how many sts to CO, divide the circumference of the shade by 2.25. Round that number to the nearest whole number, then multiply by 6 (number of stitches per repeat of the lace pattern).

Circumference of shade ÷ 2.25 x 6 = Number of CO sts

To calculate how many rows to work to get the right cover height, divide the height of the shade by the row gauge.

Shade height ÷ 3.5 (row gauge) = number of pattern repeats

Round to the nearest ½"/1.3cm. If you still need to add additional length, just purl extra rows at the top and bottom. Keep in mind that knitted fabric is wonderfully stretchy in both width and length for flexibility in adjusting your cover over the shade.

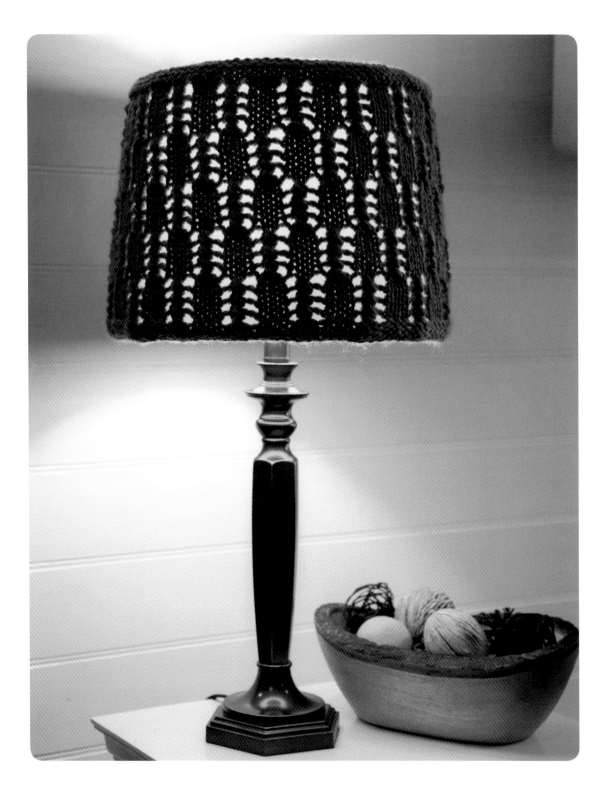

HOOP EARRINGS

Have a pair of hoop earrings that you don't wear anymore? Is there a little pile of beloved, leftover scrap yarn in your stash just waiting to be used? Repurpose both with this easy peasy project that can be completed in just a few minutes.

Skill Level: Easy   Design by: Ashley Little

MATERIALS AND TOOLS

- Oddments of bulky or super bulky weight yarn 🄻 or 🄼

- Knitting needles: double pointed needles suitable to your oddments' weights

- Earring findings: 30mm nickel-free hoops, color silver

- 2¼"/7cm giant kidney wire, color gold—or earring hoops from your jewelry box

- Tapestry needle

GAUGE

- Gauge is not important for this project.

instructions

CO 3 sts, leaving about a 3"/8cm tail. Work in I-cord (page 117) until you've knitted a cord long enough to fit around your earring's hoop, leaving a small amount of space on each side for fastening the earring to your ear.

Break yarn but do not BO.

FINISHING

Slide the I-cord through the earring hoop. With tapestry needle, run yarn tail through rem 3 sts and pull taut. Thread tapestry needle with CO tail. Run tail around the CO edge with a running stitch (page 120) and pull taut. Secure and weave in both ends.

Note: If you are using an earring with a thick post or if the I-cord does not slide easily onto the earring, you can knit the I-cord over the earring. Simply CO, knit one row, then slide the hoop into the beginning of the cord. Hold onto the earring as you knit, wrapping the cord around it.

HANDLED PURSE

This bag is worked with four strands of yarn held together, making it extra chunky and quick to knit. The bag only requires three skeins of yarn, so you'll need to pull from both ends of one of the skeins to get the four strands you'll need.

Skill Level: Intermediate

Design by: Biscuitscout

MATERIALS AND TOOLS

- Elle Rustica Chunky (60% acrylic, 20% wool, 20% tweed; 1.76oz/50g = 82yds/75m); 3 skeins, color Charcoal #051—approximately 246yds/225m of bulky weight yarn (5)

- Knitting needles: 10mm (size 15 U.S.)

- Cable needle

- Tapestry needle

- 1 pair of bamboo or wooden handbag handles, 6"/15cm wide

GAUGE

- 9 sts/14 rows = 4"/10cm in St st with 4 strands of yarn held tog

SPECIAL ABBREVIATIONS

- MB (make bobble): P1, k1, p1 into next stitch, turn and k3, turn and p3, turn and k3, turn and p3tog.

- C4B (Cable 4 Back): slip next 2 stitches onto cable needle and hold at back of work, knit next 2 stitches from left-hand needle, then knit 2 stitches from cable needle.

FINISHED MEASUREMENTS

- 9¾ x 8" (25cm x 20cm) measured flat and excluding handles

instructions

BODY (MAKE 2)

With 4 strands held tog, CO 18 sts.

Row 1 (RS): P7, k4, p7.

Row 2 and all even rows (WS): K7, p4, k7.

Row 3: P4, MB, p2, C4B, p2, MB, p4.

Rows 5 and 7: Rep row 1.

Row 8: Rep Row 2.

Rep rows 3–8 three times, then rep rows 3–5 once.

BO, leaving a 50"/127cm tail to sew the handles.

FINISHING

Sew the two bottom seams together using mattress stitch (see page 119). Sew the side seams from bottom to top, stopping around 2"/5cm from the top to allow space to open your bag.

Thread the 50"/127cm tail through your tapestry needle. Wrap the yarn around the handle from front to back. Insert needle through first BO stitch and pull yarn through from back to front. Rep until you have sewn all the BO stitches. Rep for the handle on the opposite side.

Secure yarn and weave in all ends.

FINGERLESS GLOVES

These gloves use a corrugated pattern made of knit and purl rows that make the beginner-friendly texture look a little more challenging than it actually is. Break these out to transition between seasons and knit up a few extra pairs as gifts while you're at it.

Skill Level: Easy   Design by: Meghan Jones

MATERIALS AND TOOLS

* Berocco Peruvia Quick (100% wool; 3.5oz/100g = 103yds/94m); 1 skein, color Sea Turtle #9125—approximately 103yds/94m of bulky weight yarn (5)

* Knitting needles: 8mm (size 11 U.S.) double pointed needles or size to obtain gauge

* Stitch markers

* Tapestry needle

GAUGE

* 12 sts/16 rows = 4"/10cm in St st

SPECIAL ABBREVIATIONS

* M1R: From the back, lift loop between stitches with left needle, knit into front of loop

* M1L: From the front, lift loop between stitches with left needle, knit into back of loop

FINISHED MEASUREMENTS

* Sizes S (M, L): 7½ (8½, 9½)"/19 (22, 24) cm hand circumference

CORRUGATED PATTERN

* Rnds 1–3: Knit.

* Rnds 4–6: Purl.

instructions

CUFF

CO 22 (26, 30) sts, arrange on 3 dpns, pm, and join to work in the rnd, being careful not to twist sts.

Rnds 1–12: Work in Corrugated Pattern.

Rnds 13–15: Knit around.

Rnd 16: Purl around.

F

Rnd 1: K around.

Rnd 2: *K1, p1; rep from * 4 (5, 6) times, pm, k1, pm, *p1, k1; rep from * to last st, p1.

Rnd 3: Continue in pattern to marker, sm, M1R, k to marker, M1L, sm, work in pattern to end—24 (28, 32) sts.

Rnd 4: Work even, working sts as they appear.

Rep Gussett Rnds 3 and 4 two (two, three) more times, then work Rnd 3 once more—30 (34, 38) sts.

Sizes M and L only: Work 2 rnds even, continuing pattern as established.

All Sizes: Work in pattern to marker, sm, p to marker, sm, work in pattern to end.

SHAPING

Next Rnd: Work in pattern to marker, sm, BO 9 (9, 11) sts loosely, removing 2nd marker. Work in pattern to end.

Next (inc) Rnd: Work in pattern to marker, sm, CO 2 sts using the Backwards Loop Method (page 114), work in pattern to end.

Next (dec) Rnd: Work in pattern to marker, remove marker, k2tog, work to end in pattern.

Cont even in pattern until piece measures 3½ (4½, 5½)"/9 (11, 14)cm from beginning of Gusset.

Next Rnd: Knit around.

Next Rnd: Purl around.

BO all sts loosely knitwise.

FINISHING

Weave in all ends. Block lightly (page 120), using steam to neaten ribbing.

POINTED GARTER
WINDOW VALANCE

POINTED GARTER WINDOW VALANCE

This valance is an easy way to add a cozy look to your windows. The stitch is a simple lace pattern, knit sideways, so you can easily repeat the pattern until you get the width you need to cover your window.

Skill Level: Intermediate   Design by: Julie Finocchiaro

MATERIALS AND TOOLS

- Lion Brand Wool Ease Thick & Quick (80% acrylic, 20% wool; 6oz/170g = 106yds/97m); 1 skein, color Glacier #640-105—approximately 106yds/97m of super bulky weight yarn 🄺

- Knitting needles: 9 mm (size 13 U.S) circular needle or size to obtain gauge; Spare 10mm (size 15 U.S.) for casting on

- Tapestry needle

- 1"/2.5cm diameter curtain rod

GAUGE

- 9 sts/16 rows = 4"/10cm in Garter Stitch using smaller needles

SPECIAL ABBREVIATION

- k3tog = knit the next three sts tog

FINISHED MEASUREMENTS

- 37" wide x 11" high (94cm x 28cm)

instructions

With larger spare needle, CO 24 sts using the Long-Tail method (see page 113).

Change to smaller needle.

Row 1 (WS): K18, p6.

Row 2 (RS): K6, yo, k2tog, k2, yo, k2tog, yo, skp, k3, yo, skp, k3, yo, k2tog.

Row 3: K18, p6.

Row 4: K6, yo, k2tog, k3, yo, k2tog, yo, (skp, k3, yo) twice, k1.

Row 5: K19, p6.

Row 6: K6, yo, k2tog, k4, yo, k2tog, yo, (skp, k3, yo) twice, k1.

Row 7: K20, p6.

Row 8: K6, yo, K2tog, K5, yo, K2tog, yo, (skp, k3, yo) twice, k1.

Row 9: K21, p6.

Row 10: K6, yo, K2tog, K6, yo, K2tog, yo, (skp, k3, yo) twice, k1.

Row 11: K22, p6.

Row 12: K6, yo, K2tog, K7, yo, K2tog, yo, (skp, k3, yo) twice, k1.

Row 13: K23, p6.

Row 14: K6, yo, k2tog, k4, (k2tog, yo) twice, (k3, k2tog, yo) twice, k3tog.

Row 15: K21, p6.

Row 16: K6, yo, k2tog, k3, (k2tog, yo) twice, k3, k2tog, yo, k2tog, k3, yo, k2tog.

Row 17: K20, p6.

Row 18: K6, yo, k2tog, k2, (k2tog, yo) twice, k3, k2tog, yo, k2tog, k3, yo, k2tog.

Row 19: K19, p6.

Row 20: K6, yo, k2tog, k1, (k2tog, yo) twice, k3, k2tog, yo, k2tog, k3, yo, k2tog.

Repeat rows 1–20 until valance is just slightly longer than the length of the curtain rod. End with row 20 to keep pattern even along lower edge of valance.

Next row: Rep Row 1.

BO kwise.

FINISHING

With yarn and a tapestry needle, fold the top edge just above the first row of yos to the back of valance to create a pocket for the curtain rod. Sew using a running stitch (page 120) along the entire edge. Weave in all ends. Slide the curtain rod through the pocket, being careful not to snag the yarn.

If you find that the pointed edges of your valance are curling a bit, block the valance (page 120) to make it lie flat.

BUTTONED COLLAR COWL

You just need one skein of yarn and a couple of hours to knit up this collar cowl. Wear it as an indoor accessory with a pretty top or bundle it up over your coat for extra warmth.

Skill Level: Easy   Design by: Adrienne Krey

MATERIALS AND TOOLS

- Brown Sheep Burly Spun (100% wool; 7.97oz/226g = 132yds/121m); 1 skein, color Oregano #113—approximately 132yds/121m of super bulky weight yarn (6)

- Knitting needles: 10mm (size 15 U.S.) or size to obtain gauge

- Tapestry needle

- Sewing needle and thread

- 1 large button (Adrienne used a 1¾"/4.4cm button)

GAUGE

- 8 sts/10 rows = 4"/10cm in Garter st

SPECIAL ABBREVIATION

- Kfb: Knit in the front and back of the same stitch

FINISHED MEASUREMENTS

- 43"/109cm in length, 10"/25cm wide at widest point

instructions

CO 6 sts.

Rows 1-2: Knit.
Row 3: Kfb, k5—7 sts.
Row 4 (and all even rows): Knit.
Row 5: Kfb, k6—8 sts.
Row 7: Kfb, k7—9 sts.
Row 9: Kfb, k8—10 sts.
Row 11: Kfb, k9—11 sts.
Row 13: Kfb, k10—12 sts.
Row 15: Kfb, k11—13 sts.
Row 17: Kfb, k12—14 sts.
Row 19: Kfb, k13—15 sts.
Row 21: Kfb, k14—16 sts.
Row 23: Kfb, k15—17 sts.
Row 25: Kfb, k16—18 sts.
Row 27: Kfb, k17—19 sts.
Row 29: Kfb, k18—20 sts.
Rows 30-70: Knit.
Row 71: Ssk, k18—19 sts.
Row 72 (and all even rows): Knit.
Row 73: Ssk, k17—18 sts.

Row 75 (Buttonhole Row): Ssk, k9, yo, k2tog, k5—17 sts.
Row 77: Ssk, k15—16 sts.
Row 79: Ssk, k14—15 sts.
Row 81: Ssk, k13—14 sts.
Row 83: Ssk, k12—13 sts.
Row 85: Ssk, k11—12 sts.
Row 87: Ssk, k10—11 sts.
Row 89: Ssk, k9—10 sts.
Row 91: Ssk, k8—9 sts.
Row 93: Ssk, k7—8 sts.
Row 95: Ssk, k6—7 sts.
Row 97: Ssk, k5—6 sts.
Rows 98 and 99: Knit.
BO.

FINISHING

Weave in all ends. Fold wrap in half lengthwise. Sew on button in the same location as the buttonhole but on the opposite side of the cowl.

Cowl should be worn buttoned with the shaped edge folded over to create the collar.

FRINGED KERCHIEF

Give a neutral yarn a few bright (or even neon!) pops of color with a kerchief that's easy to knit and construct. The seam at the back ensures the kerchief drapes perfectly without sliding off your shoulders, and the fringe offers additional opportunity to play with color and texture.

Skill Level: Easy   Design by: Adrienne Krey

MATERIALS AND TOOLS

◆ Knit Picks Billow (100% pima cotton; 3.5oz/100g = 120yds/110m): (A), 1 skein, color Ash #26233; 1 skein, color Tea Rose #26228 (B)—approximately 240yds/219m of bulky weight yarn (5)

◆ Knitting needles: 6.5mm (size 10½ U.S.) circular needle, 29"/74cm long

◆ Crochet hook: 5mm (size H-8 U.S.) crochet hook, for fringe (optional)

◆ Tapestry needle

GAUGE

◆ 13 sts/16 rows = 4"/10cm in St st

FINISHED MEASUREMENTS

◆ Approx 40"/102cm in length

instructions

With A, CO 64 sts.

Work in St st until piece measures approx 12"/30.5cm from CO edge, ending with a WS row.

Rows 1 & 2: With B, work in St st.

Rows 3 & 4: Change to A. Cont in St st.

Rows 5–8: Change to B. Cont in St st.

Rows 9–12: Change to A. Cont in St st.

Break A. With B, continue working in St st until piece measures approx 24"/61cm from CO edge, ending with a WS row. BO.

FINISHING

Fold work diagonally by bringing the bottom left corner of your knit rectangle to meet the upper right corner. Use a mattress stitch (page 119) to seam a 9"/23cm seam that forms the kerchief.

Weave in all ends.

For the optional fringe, cut 26 lengths of yarn in each color, approx 16"/41cm in length. Using 2 strands of each color (4 strands total), fold yarn in half and use crochet hook to pull loop through the edge of the scarf. Then, pull the strands through that loop and pull downward to tighten.

Attach fringe at regular intervals along the open unseamed edges of the scarf.

BRAIDED
WALL ART

Let your yarn love take the spotlight with this pretty framed piece. An eye-catching braided cable and soft bulky yarn bring color and texture to any room, and with versatile instructions, you can create this project to fit any dimension. Use a natural wooden frame and neutral yarns to lend subtle warmth to a space, or go bold with saturated hues and a bright contrasting frame for a scene-stealing show.

Skill Level: Easy   Design by: Katie Worthing

MATERIALS AND TOOLS

- Alafoss Lopi (100% new wool; 3.5oz/100g = 109yds/100m); 1 skein, color Light Indigo #9958—approximately 109yds/100m of bulky weight yarn (5)

- Knitting needles: 8mm (size 11 U.S.) or size to obtain gauge

- Cable needle

- Tapestry needle

- 14" x 11" (36cm x 28cm) standard frame

- Lightweight spray adhesive

GAUGE

- 12 sts and 16 rows= 4"/10cm in Reverse St st

SPECIAL ABBREVIATIONS

- C6B: Slip the next 3 sts onto cable needle and hold behind your work, k the next 3 sts, k3 from the cable needle

- C6F: Slip the next 3 sts onto cable needle and hold in front of your work, k the next 3 sts, k3 from the cable needle

FINISHED MEASUREMENTS

- To fit 14" x 11" (36cm x 28cm) standard frame, oriented vertically. Project can be resized to fit other frames; please see instructions.

instructions

PANEL

CO 34 sts.

Row 1 (RS): P11, k12, p11.

Row 2 and all even rows (WS): K11, p12, k11.

Row 3: P11, C6B, C6F, p11.

Row 5: Rep Row 1.

Rep rows 1–6 eight more times.

BO loosely.

RESIZE WIDTH OF PANEL

If you are using a frame larger or smaller than 14" x 11" (36cm x 28cm), use the chart on the next page to add or subtract sts on each side of the cable.

Frame Width	CO	Sts on each side of cable
17"/43cm	52 sts	20 sts
16"/41cm	50 sts	19 sts
15"/38cm	46 sts	17 sts
14"/36cm	44 sts	16 sts
13"/33cm	40 sts	14 sts
12"/30.5cm	38 sts	13 sts
10"/25cm	30 sts	9 sts
9"/23cm	28 sts	8 sts
8"/20cm	24 sts	6 sts
7"/18cm	22 sts	5 sts
6"/15cm	18 sts	3 sts
5"/13cm	16 sts	2 sts

RESIZE HEIGHT OF PANEL

Rep rows 1–6 until the piece measures desired frame height. End on a WS row. BO.

FINISHING

Weave in ends.

Lightly block (page 120) the piece to frame measurements, being careful not to flatten cable, and allow to dry.

Remove frame backing from frame. Lightly coat the frame backing with an even layer of spray adhesive.

Lay the knit piece onto the backing, adjusting it to match dimensions. Evenly smooth the knitting, keeping the cable centered and making sure the piece covers the entire backing and is fully adhered. Secure the backing into the frame and hang.

MELEGRANA HAT

MELEGRANA HAT

Maria calls her beautiful lace design *melagrana*, the Italian word for "pomegranate." With its round, fruit-like pattern and the pretty yarn-overs that look like seeds, the luscious fruit parallel is striking. This hat is worked in a firmer gauge to hold the classic shape of the pillbox, and you can find a matching pattern in Maria's gorgeous Melagrana Capelet on page 97.

Skill Level: Intermediate   Design by: Maria Näslund

MATERIALS AND TOOLS

◆ Brown Sheep Company Lamb's Pride Superwash Bulky (100% wool; 3.5oz/100g = 110yds/101m); 1 skein, Frosted Fuchsia #SWB165, —approximately 110yds/101m bulky weight yarn 🅵

◆ Knitting needles: 5mm (size 8 U.S.) circular and double pointed needles or size needed to obtain gauge

◆ Stitch markers

◆ Stitch holders or waste yarn

GAUGE

◆ 14 sts/24 rows = 4"/10cm in top pattern

SPECIAL ABBREVIATIONS

◆ cdd (center double decrease): sl 2 sts tog as if to k, k1, pass slipped sts over

◆ k3tog: k three together

◆ sssk: sl 3 sts individually as if to k, then k those 3 sts together through the back of the loops

FINISHED MEASUREMENTS

◆ Brim circumference: 20"/51cm

◆ Circumference at widest point: 27½"/70cm

◆ To fit head circumference: 22–23"/56–58cm

instructions

HAT

CO 15 sts provisionally with waste yarn (page 114).

BRIM

Join yarn to work brim.

BRIM PATTERN

(chart on page 95)

Row 1 and all odd rows: P12, k3.

Row 2 : K5, k2tog, (k1, yo) twice, k1, ssk, k3.

Row 4: K4, k2tog, k1, yo, k3, yo, k1, ssk, k2.

Row 6: K3, k2tog, k1, yo, k2tog, yo, k1, yo, ssk, yo, k1, ssk, k1.

Row 8: K4, (ssk, yo) twice, k1, (yo, k2tog) twice, k2.

Row 10: K4, yo, k1, ssk, k3, k2tog, k1, yo, k2.

Row 12: K5, yo, k1, ssk, k1, k2tog, k1, yo, k3.

Row 14: K4, yo, ssk, yo, k1, sk2p, k1, yo, k2tog, yo, k2.

Row 16: K6, yo, k2tog, k1, ssk, yo, k4.

Rows 1–16 form pattern.

Work Rows 1–16 of the Brim pattern 6 times, then work Rows 1–15 once. Undo the provisional cast on and place sts on a needle. Graft the CO end together in pattern, knitting Row 16 and forming a circle.

TOP

Pick up and k 104 sts along the top edge of the brim, skipping a st between sts 14 and 15. Pick up 13 sts, skipping the 14th, and so on.

Note: There will be 4 pattern repeats in one rnd.

TOP PATTERN

(chart on page 95)

Rnd 1: *P1, k1, ssk, k1, yo, k1, sk2p, k1, yo, k1, k2tog, k1, p1, k2, k2tog, (k1, yo) twice, k1, ssk, k2; rep from * around—96 sts

Rnd 2 and all even rnds: Work sts as they appear, knitting the yo sts.

Rnd 3: *P1, k2, k2tog, (k1, yo) twice, k1, ssk, k2, p1, k1, k2tog, k1, yo, k3, yo, k1, ssk, k1; rep from * around.

Rnd 5: *P1, k3tog, k1, yo, k3, yo, k1, sssk, p1, k2tog, k1, yo, k2tog, yo, k1, yo, ssk, yo, k1, ssk; rep from * around—88 sts.

Rnd 7: *P1, (ssk, yo) twice, k1, (yo, k2tog) twice, p1, k1, (ssk, yo) twice, k1, (yo, k2tog) twice, k1; rep from * around.

Rnd 9: *P1, k1, ssk, k3, k2tog, k1, p1, k1, yo, k1, ssk, k3, k2tog, k1, yo, k1; rep from * around—80 sts.

Rnd 11: *P1, k1, ssk, k1, k2tog, k1, p1, k2, yo, k1, ssk, k1, k2tog, k1, yo, k2; rep from * around—72 sts.

Rnd 13: *P1, k1, sk2p, k1, p1, k1, yo, ssk, yo, k1, sk2p, k1, yo, k2tog, yo, k1; rep from * around—64 sts.

Rnd 15: *P1, sk2p, p1, k2, k2tog, k1, yo, k1, yo, k1, ssk, k2; rep from * around—56 sts.

Rnd 17: P1, *p1, (k2tog) twice, k1, yo, k3, yo, k1, (ssk) twice; rep from * around. First st of the rnd is consumed by the last st of the rnd—48 sts.

Rnd 19: *P1, cdd, yo, ssk, yo, k1, yo, k2tog, yo, cdd; rep from * around—40 sts.

Rnd 21: *P1, k1, ssk, k3, k2tog, k1; rep from * around—32 sts.

Rnd 23: *P1, k1, ssk, k1, k2tog, k1; rep from * around—24 sts.

Rnd 25: *P1, k1, sk2p, k1; rep from * around—16 sts.

Rnd 27: *P1, sk2p; rep from * around—8 sts.

FINISHING

Pull yarn through the remaining sts and weave in the ends.

To emphazise the pillbox shape when blocking, place a flat plate about 8¼"/21cm in diameter on top of a somewhat smaller cylinder such as a jar. Block the hat over the plate, pulling gently into shape to open up the lace on the top.

MELEGRANA HAT

BRIM CHART

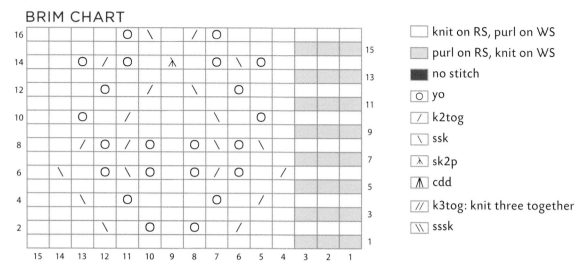

Legend:
- ☐ knit on RS, purl on WS
- ▨ purl on RS, knit on WS
- ■ no stitch
- O yo
- / k2tog
- \ ssk
- λ sk2p
- Λ cdd
- // k3tog: knit three together
- \\ sssk

On Rnd 17, the stitch within the red box is only worked once. As the first stitch of the rnd, it will be consumed by the last st of the rnd.

TOP CHART

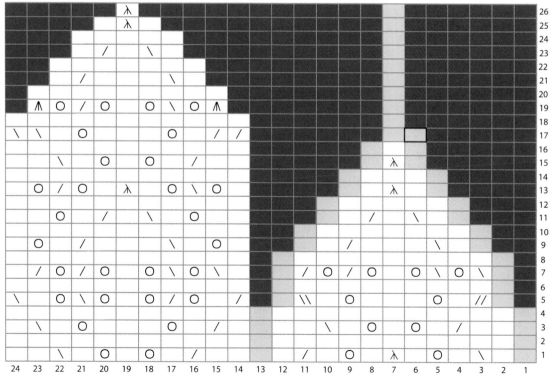

MELEGRANA CAPELET

This stunning capelet is worked at a looser gauge to make sure it's a soft and cozy garment. If you want to keep your head warm, too, you'll find the matching hat pattern on page 92.

Skill Level: Advanced

Design by: Maria Näslund

MATERIALS AND TOOLS

- Brown Sheep Company Lamb's Pride Superwash Bulky (100% wool; 3.5oz/100g = 110yds/101m); 3 (3, 4, 5) skeins, Finches #SWB53, approximately 330 (330, 440, 550)yds/302 (302, 402, 503)m of bulky weight yarn (5)

- Knitting needles: 6mm (size 10 U.S.) circular needle, 30"/76cm long or size needed to obtain gauge

- Stitch markers

- Stitch holders or waste yarn

GAUGE

- 10 sts/16 rows = 4"/10cm in stockinette

- 10 sts/16 rows = 4"/10cm in lace rib pattern

- 14 sts/16 rows = 5 x 4" (13 x10 cm) in one rep of lace rib

SPECIAL ABBREVIATION

- sskp: sl1 kwise, sl1 pwise, k those 2 slipped sts together, pass next st over

FINISHED MEASUREMENTS

- XS/S (M/L, XL/2XL, 3XL/4XL), shown in size M/L

- Length: 14½ (15, 15½, 16)"/37 (38, 39.5, 40.5)cm

- Neck width: 17 (18½, 20, 21½)"/43 (47, 51, 55)cm

- Bottom width: 48 (53, 58, 63)"/122 (135, 147.5, 160)cm

instructions

CO 133 (149, 165, 181) sts.

Row 1: Purl.

Row 2: P4, k1, pm, p to last 5 sts, pm, k1, p4.

Begin working Border pattern

BORDER PATTERN
(chart on page 102)

Row 1 (RS): P5, sm, *k2, k2tog, (k1, yo) twice, k1, ssk, k2, ssk, k1, k2tog; rep from * 6 (7, 8, 9) times, k2, k2tog, (k1, yo) twice, k1, ssk, k2, sm, p5—119 (133, 147, 161) sts.

Even rows 2–6 (WS): P4, k1, sm, work sts as they appear to marker (p the yo sts), sm, k1, p4.

Row 3: P5, sm, *k1, k2tog, k1, yo, k3, yo, k1, ssk, k4; rep from * 6 (7, 8, 9) times, k1, k2tog, k1, yo, k3, yo, k1, sm, p5.

Row 5: P5, sm, *k2tog, k1, yo, k2tog, yo, k1, yo, ssk, yo, k1, ssk, k3; rep from * 6 (7, 8, 9) times, k2tog, k1, yo, k2tog, yo, k1, yo, ssk, yo, k1, ssk, sm, p5.

Row 7: P5, sm, *k1, (ssk, yo) twice, k1, (yo, k2tog) twice, k1, yo, sk2p, yo; rep from * 6 (7, 8, 9) times, k1, (ssk, yo) twice, k1, (yo, k2tog) twice, k1, sm, p5.

Even rows 8–16 (WS): P4, k1, sm, p11, *k3, p11; rep from *6 (7, 8, 9) times, sm, k1, p4.

Row 9: P5, sm, *k1, yo, k1, ssk, k3, k2tog, k1, yo, k1, p3; rep from * 6 (7, 8, 9) times, k1, yo, k1, ssk, k3, k2tog, k1, yo, k1, sm, p5.

Row 11: P5, sm, *k2, yo, k1, ssk, k1, k2tog, k1, yo, k2, p3; rep from * 6 (7, 8, 9) times, k2, yo, k1, ssk, k1, k2tog, k1, yo, k2, sm, p5.

Row 13: P5, sm, *k1, yo, ssk, yo, k1, sk2p, k1, yo, k2tog, yo, k1, p3; rep from * 6 (7, 8, 9) times, k1, yo, ssk, yo, k1, sk2p, k1, yo, k2tog, yo, k1, sm, p5.

Row 15: P5, sm, *k3, yo, k2tog, k1, ssk, yo, k3, p3; rep from *6 (7, 8, 9) times, k3, yo, k2tog, k1, ssk, yo, k3, sm, p5.

When Border is complete, begin Lace Rib.

LACE RIB (chart on page 102)

Row 1 (RS): P5, sm, *k2, k2tog, (k1, yo) twice, k1, ssk, k2, p3; repeat from * 6 (7, 8, 9) times, k2, k2tog, (k1, yo) twice, k1, ssk, k2, sm, p5.

Row 2 and all even rows (WS): P4, k1, sm, work sts as they appear (p the yo sts) to marker, sm, k1, p4.

Row 3: P5, sm, *k1, k2tog, k1, yo, k3, yo, k1, ssk, k1, p3; repeat from * 6 (7, 8, 9) times, k1, k2tog, k1, yo, k3, yo, k1, sm, p5.

Row 5: P5, sm, *k2tog, k1, yo, k2tog, yo, k1, yo, ssk, yo, k1, ssk, p3; repeat from * 6 (7, 8, 9) times, k2tog, k1, yo, k2tog, yo, k1, yo, ssk, yo, k1, ssk, sm, p5.

Row 7: P5, sm, *k1, (ssk, yo) twice, k1, (yo, k2tog) twice, k1, p3; repeat from * 6 (7, 8, 9) times, k1, (ssk, yo) twice, k1, (yo, k2tog) twice, k1, sm, p5.

Row 9: P5, sm, *k1, yo, k1, ssk, k3, k2tog, k1, yo, k1, p3; repeat from * 6 (7, 8, 9) times, k1, yo, k1, ssk, k3, k2tog, k1, yo, k1, sm, p5.

Row 11: P5, sm, *k2, yo, k1, ssk, k1, k2tog, k1, yo, k2, p3; repeat from * 6 (7, 8, 9) times, k2, yo, k1, ssk, k1, k2tog, k1, yo, k2, sm, p5.

Row 13: P5, sm, *k1, yo, ssk, yo, k1, sk2p, k1, yo, k2tog, yo, k1, p3; repeat from * 6 (7, 8, 9) times, k1, yo, ssk, yo, k1, sk2p, k1, yo, k2tog, yo, k1, sm, p5.

Row 15: P5, sm, *k3, yo, k2tog, k1, ssk, yo, k3, p3; repeat from *6 (7, 8, 9) times, k3, yo, k2tog, k1, ssk, yo, k3, sm, p5.

Row 16: Rep Row 2.

Rep Rows 1–8 (1–10, 1–10, 1–12).

When Lace Rib is complete, work the shoulder pattern.

SHOULDER PATTERN
(chart on page 103)

Sizes XS/S and M/L

Row 1 (RS): P5, sm, *ssk, yo, k1, ssk, k1, k2tog, k1, yo, k2tog, p3; repeat from * 6 (7) times, ssk, yo, k1, ssk, k1, k2tog, k1, yo, k2tog, sm, p5.

Row 2 and all even rows (WS): P4, k1, sm, work sts as they appear (p the yo sts) to marker, sm, k1, p4.

Row 3: P5, sm, *k2, yo, k1, sk2p, k1, yo, k2, p3; repeat from * 6 (7) times, k2, yo, k1, sk2p, k1, yo, k2, sm, p5.

Row 5: P5, sm, *sskp, [k1, yo] twice, k1, sk2p, p3; repeat from * 6 (7) times, sskp, k1, yo, k1, yo, k1, sk2p, sm, p5.

Row 7: P5, sm, * k2tog, yo, k3, yo, ssk, p3; repeat from * 6 (7) times, k2tog, yo, k3, yo, ssk, sm, p5.

Row 9: p5, sm, * ssk, yo, sk2p, yo, k2tog, p3; repeat from * 6 (7) times, ssk, yo, sk2p, yo, k2tog, sm, p5.

Row 11: P5, sm, *k2, yo, ssk, k1, p3; repeat from * 6 (7) times, k2, yo, ssk, k1, sm, p5.

Row 13: P5, sm, * k2tog, k1, ssk, p3; repeat from * 6 (7) times, k2tog, k1, ssk, sm, p5.

Row 14: Rep Row 2.

Sizes XL/2XL

Row 1 (RS): P5, sm, *ssk, yo, k1, ssk, k1, k2tog, k1, yo, k2tog, p3; repeat from * 8 times, ssk, yo, k1, ssk, k1, k2tog, k1, yo, k2tog, sm, p5.

Row 2 and all even rows (WS): P4, k1, sm, work sts as they appear (p the yo sts) to marker, sm, k1, p4.

Row 3: P5, sm, *k2, yo, k1, sk2p, k1, yo, k2, p3; repeat from * 8 times, k2, yo, k1, sk2p, k1, yo, k2, sm, p5.

Row 5: P5, sm, * k1, k2tog, [k1, yo] twice, k1, ssk, k1, p3; repeat from * 8 times, k1, k2tog, k1, yo, k1, yo, k1, ssk, k1, sm, p5.

Row 7: P5, sm, *sskp, yo, k3, yo, sk2p, p3; repeat from * 8 times, sskp, yo, k3, yo, sk2p, sm, p5.

Row 9: P5, sm, * ssk, yo, k3, yo, k2tog, p3; repeat from * 8 times, ssk, yo, k3, yo, k2tog, sm, p5.

Row 11: p5, sm, * ssk, yo, sk2p, yo, k2tog, p3; repeat from * 8 times, ssk, yo, sk2p, yo, k2tog, sm, p5.

Row 13: P5, sm, *k2, yo, ssk, k1, p3; repeat from * 8 times, k2, yo, ssk, k1, sm, p5.

Row 15: P5, sm, * k2tog, k1, ssk, p3; repeat from * 8 times, k2tog, k1, ssk, sm, p5.

Row 16: Rep Row 2.

Sizes 3XL/4XL

Row 1 (RS): P5, sm, *ssk, k1, yo, k1, sk2p, k1, yo, k1, k2tog, p3; repeat from * 9 times, ssk, k1, yo, k1, sk2p, k1, yo, k1, k2tog, sm, p5.

Row 2 and all even rows (WS): P4, k1, sm, work sts as they appear (p the yo sts) to marker, sm, k1, p4.

Row 3: P5, sm, *k2, yo, k2tog, k1, ssk, yo, k2, p3; repeat from * 9 times, k2, yo, k2tog, k1, ssk, yo, k2, sm, p5.

Row 5: P5, sm, * k1, k2tog, (k1, yo) twice, k1, ssk, k1, p3; repeat from * 8 times, k1, k2tog, k1, yo, k1, yo, k1, ssk, k1, sm, p5.

Row 7: P5, sm, *sskp, yo, k3, yo, sk2p, p3; repeat from * 8 times, sskp, yo, k3, yo, sk2p, sm, p5.

Row 9: P5, sm, * ssk, yo, k3, yo, k2tog, p3; repeat from * 8 times, ssk, yo, k3, yo, k2tog, sm, p5.

Row 11: P5, sm, * ssk, yo, sk2p, yo, k2tog, p3; repeat from * 8 times, ssk, yo, sk2p, yo, k2tog, sm, p5.

Row 13: P5, sm, *k2, yo, ssk, k1, p3; repeat from * 8 times, k2, yo, ssk, k1, sm, p5.

Row 15: P5, sm, * k2tog, k1, ssk, p3; repeat from * 8 times, k2tog, k1, ssk, sm, p5.

Row 16: Rep Row 2.

NECK SHAPING

Next Row (RS): P5, sm, k2, *ssk, p1, k2tog, k1; repeat from * to 1 st bef marker, k1, sm, p5—41 (45, 49, 53) sts.

Put the sts on a piece of waste yarn or stitch holder.

COLLAR

CO 61 (61, 71, 71) sts.

Next row: Purl.

Next row: P4, k1, pm, p to last 5 sts, pm, k1, p4.

Begin working the collar pattern.

COLLAR PATTERN
(chart on page 102)

Row 1 (RS): P5, sm, k2, k2tog, k1, yo, k1, *yo, k1, ssk, k3, k2tog, k1, yo, k1; repeat from * 3 (3, 4, 4) times, yo, k1, ssk, k2, sm, p5.

Row 2 and all even rows (WS): P4, k1, sm, work sts as they appear (p the yo sts) to marker, sm, k1, p4.

Row 3: P5, sm, k1, k2tog, k1, yo, k2, *k1, yo, k1, ssk, k1, k2tog, k1, yo, k2; repeat from * 3 (3, 4, 4) times, k1, yo, k1, ssk, k1, sm, p5.

Row 5: P5, sm, ssk, k1, yo, k2tog, yo, k1, *yo, ssk, yo, k1, sk2p, k1, yo, k2tog, yo, k1; repeat from * 3 (3, 4, 4) times, yo, ssk, yo, k1, k2tog, sm, p5.

Row 7: P5, sm, k1, (ssk, yo) twice, k1, * (yo, k2tog) twice, k1, [ssk, yo] twice, k1; repeat from * 3 (3, 4, 4) times, (yo, k2tog) twice, k1, sm, p5.

Row 9: P5, sm, k1, yo, k1, ssk, k2, *k1, k2tog, (k1, yo) twice, k1, ssk, k2; repeat from * 3 (3, 4, 4) times, k1, k2tog, k1, yo, k1, sm, p5.

Row 11: P5, sm, ssk, yo, k1, ssk, k1, *k2tog, k1, yo, sk2p, yo, k1, ssk, k1; repeat from * 3 (3, 4, 4) times, k2tog, k1, yo, k2tog, sm, p5—51 (51, 59, 59) sts.

Row 12: Rep Row 2.

XS/S only
Row 13: P5, sm, ssk, yo, k1, sk2p, * k1, yo, k2tog, yo, k1, sk2p; repeat from * 3 times, k1, yo, k2tog, sm, p5—41 sts.

M/L only
Row 13: P5, sm, ssk, yo, k1, sk2p, (k1, yo, k1, ssk, yo, k1, sk2p) twice, (k1, yo, k2tog, k1, yo, k1, sk2p) twice, k1, yo, k2tog, sm, p5—45 sts.

XL/2XL only
Row 13: P5, sm, ssk, yo, k1, sk2p, (k1, yo, k2tog, yo, k1, sk2p) twice, k1, yo, k3, yo, k1, sk2p, (k1, yo, k2tog, yo, k1, sk2p) twice, k1, yo, k2tog, sm, p5—49 sts.

3XL/4XL only
Row 13: P5, sm, ssk, yo, k1, sk2p, (k1, yo, k1, ssk, yo, k1, sk2p) twice, k1, yo, k3, yo, k1, sk2p, (k1, yo, k2tog, k1, yo, k1, sk2p) twice, k1, yo, k2tog, sm, p5—53 sts.

COLLAR SHAPING

The neck part of the collar is shaped with short rows, to allow it to lie nice and flat.

Next row (WS): P4, k1, p20 (23, 26, 29), turn.

Next row (RS): Yo btf, k9 (11 13, 15) turn.

Next row: Yo, p to yo, ssp, p6 (8, 10, 12), turn.

Next row: Yo btf, k to yo, k2tog, k6 (8, 10, 12), turn.

Next row: Yo, p to yo, ssp, p until 5 sts rem, k1, p4.

Next row: P5, k to yo, k2tog, k until 5 sts rem, p5.

JOINING THE COLLAR

Put the held sts of the capelet on a needle. Put the collar on top of the capelet, both with WS facing, needles parallel to each other. Join capelet and collar with a three needle bind-off (see page 116).

FINISHING

Weave in the ends and block (page 120) to measurements.

CAPELET BORDER CHART

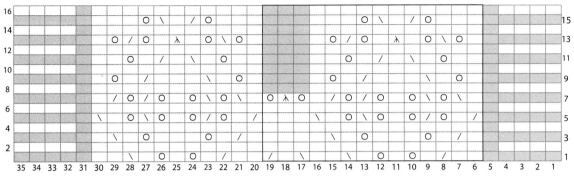

CAPELET LACE RIB CHART

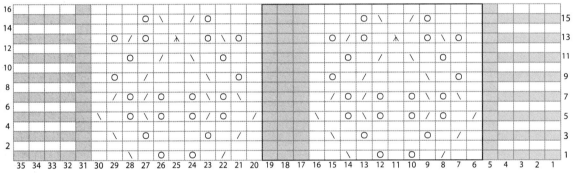

CAPELET COLLAR CHART

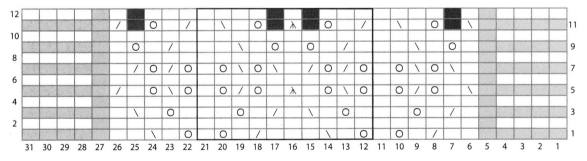

CAPELET SHOULDER CHART, XS/S AND M/L

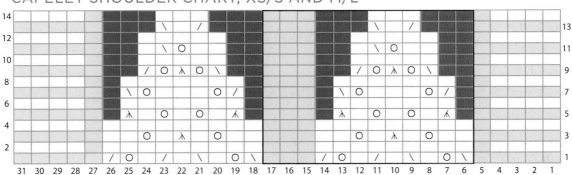

CAPELET SHOULDER CHART, XL/2XL

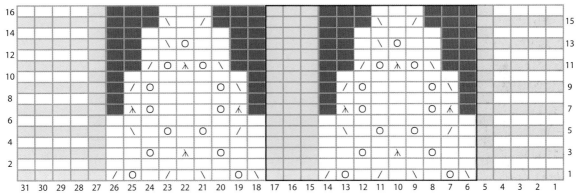

CAPELET SHOULDER CHART, 3XL/4XL

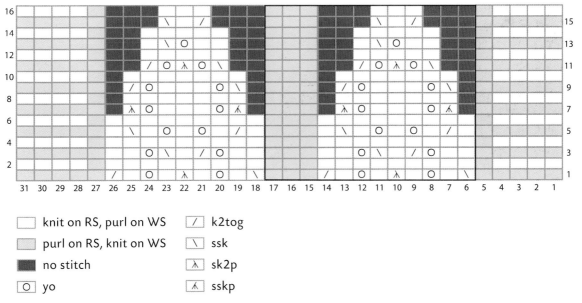

	knit on RS, purl on WS		/	k2tog
	purl on RS, knit on WS		\	ssk
	no stitch		人	sk2p
O	yo		人	sskp

SCALLOP PARTY NECKLACE

When it comes to knitted jewelry, lightweight yarns shouldn't get all the glory. Show off the stitch definition of bulky yarn with this pretty piece of eye candy. A basic crochet slip stitch finishes off the top and adds even more color.

Skill Level: Easy   Design by: Adrienne Krey

MATERIALS AND TOOLS

- Berroco Vintage Chunky (52% acrylic, 40% wool, 8% nylon; 3.5oz/100g = 130yds/120m); 1 skein each Bilberry #61104 (A), Wasabi #6165 (B), and Minty #6112 (C)—approximately 40yds/36.5m total of bulky weight yarn (5)

- Knitting needles: 6mm (size 10 U.S.) straight needles or size to obtain gauge

- Crochet hook: 6mm (size J-10 U.S.)

- Tapestry needle

- Sewing needle and thread

- 1 medium-sized button (Adrienne used a ¾"/1.9cm button)

GAUGE

- 14 sts/20 rows = 4"/10cm in Garter st

SPECIAL ABBREVIATION

- Kfb: Knit in the front and back of the same stitch

FINISHED MEASUREMENTS

- Approx 20"/51cm long

instructions

With A, CO 4 sts.

Work in Garter st until piece measures 6"/15cm.

SMALL SCALLOP

Row 1: SSK, k2tog—2 sts.

Row 2: Kfb into both sts—4 sts.

Rows 3, 5, 7, 9: Knit.

Row 4: Kfb, k3—5 sts.

Row 6: Kfb, k4—6 sts.

Row 8: Kfb, k5—7 sts.

Row 10: Kfb, k6—8 sts.

Row 11: K6, k2tog—7 sts.

Rows 12, 14, 16, 18: Knit.

Row 13: K5, k2tog—6 sts.

Row 15: K4, k2tog—5 sts.

Row 17: K3, k2tog—4 sts.

LARGE SCALLOP

Row 19: SSK, k2tog—2 sts.

Row 20: (Kfb) twice—4 sts.

Rows 21–31 (odd rows only): Knit.

Row 22: Kfb, k3—5 sts.

Row 24: Kfb, k4—6 sts.

Row 26: Kfb, k5—7 sts.

Row 28: Kfb, k6—8 sts.

Row 30: Kfb, k7—9 sts.

Row 32: Kfb, k8—10 sts.

Row 33: K8, k2tog—9 sts.

Rows 34-44 (even rows only): Knit.

Row 35: K7, k2tog—8 sts.

Row 37: K6, k2tog—7 sts.

Row 39: K5, k2tog—6 sts.

Row 41: K4, k2tog—5 sts.

Row 43: K3, k2tog—4 sts.

Rep Rows 1–20, then work in Garter St for approx 6"/15cm.

BUTTONHOLE

Row 1: K2, yo, k2.

Row 2: K2, k2tog, k1.

Row 3: Knit.

BO.

GARTER EDGING

Starting at the CO end of necklace, insert crochet hook between garter ridges into the first st of the row. You should insert the hook into the st on the straight edge of the necklace without the shaped scallops.

Attach B and slip st around the straight edge of the necklace until you reach the BO end.

Turn your work and repeat this process, inserting the hook into the back loop of each color B st you just worked.

Rep one more slip st row with C. Fasten off.

FINISHING

Weave in all ends.

Sew button to CO end of necklace.

SOFT SACHETS

SOFT SACHETS

These versatile sachets can perform many amazing feats. Knit them up as Christmas tree ornaments, give them away as gifts, hang them in your home for décor, or just skip the ribbon completely and scatter them in your drawers to keep everything smelling spiffy.

Skill Level: Intermediate   Design by: Megan Mannell

MATERIALS AND TOOLS

- Berroco Vintage Chunky (52% wool, 40% acrylic, 8% nylon; 3.5 oz/100g = 130yds/119m); 1 skein each of Sour Cherry #6134, Pumpkin #6176, and Black Cherry #6181—approximately 24yds/22m of bulky weight yarn for each sachet (5)

- Knitting needles: 6mm (size 10 U.S.) double pointed needles or size to obtain gauge

- Stitch marker

- Cable needle

- Fiberfill

- Scent of choice, such as dried lavender or dried pine needles

- Tapestry needle

- 8–10"/20–25cm length of thin twine or ribbon

GAUGE

- 15 sts/20 rows = 4"/10cm in pattern stitch

SPECIAL ABBREVIATIONS

- Kfb: Knit into the front and back of the same st

- C6F: Sl next 3 sts to cable needle and bring to front. K next 3 sts, then k 3 sts from the cable needle together through the back of the loops

FINISHED MEASUREMENTS

- Approximately 10"/25cm circumference at the widest point

instructions

CO 20. Pm and join into the rnd, being careful not to twist sts.

Rnd 1: *K2, p1, k1, p1; rep from * around.

Rnd 2: *(Kfb) twice, p1, k1, p1; rep from * around—28 sts.

Rnd 3: *Kfb, k2, kfb, p1, k1, p1; rep from * around—36 sts.

Rnd 4: *K6, p1, k1, p1; rep from * around.

Rnd 5: *C6F, p1, k1, p1; rep from * around.

Rep Rnd 4 five times. Rep Rnd 5 once, then rep Rnd 4 five more times.

Next rnd: Rep Rnd 5.

Next rnd: Rep Rnd 4.

Next rnd: *Ssk, k2, k2tog, p1, k1, p1; rep from * around—28 sts.

Next rnd: *Ssk, k2tog, p1, k1, p1; rep from * around—20 sts.

FINISHING

Break yarn and draw tail through the rem sts. Pull taut to cinch this end of the sachet closed. Weave in ends.

Stuff and fill the sachet with fiberfill and your scent of choice.

Thread tapestry needle with ribbon or twine. Whipstitch (page 120) into each of the stitches on the CO edge.

Tie the two ends of the ribbon or twine together. Tuck this knot inside the sachet, and pull on the loop of twine or ribbon opposite the knot in order to cinch the opening closed.

Finish this loop by knotting the ribbon or twine securely at the base of the sachet.

Note: This loop allows you to hang the sachet as an ornament. If you do not want to add a loop to your sachet, simply close the CO edge by drawing the tail end of the yarn through each st and cinching them together tightly.

HEADBAND SQUARED

This pretty square-in-a-square pattern is lovely *and* simple to knit with a repeating sequence of knits and purls, making it easy enough even for a brand new knitter. Try knitting this with two strands of bulky yarn held together for an even cozier beat-the-cold accessory.

Skill Level: Easy   Design by: Ashley Little

MATERIALS AND TOOLS

◆ Bernat Roving (80% acrylic, 20% wool; 3.53oz/100g = 120yds/110m); 1 skein, Low Tide #00098—approximately 120yds/110m of bulky weight yarn (5)

◆ Knitting needles: 8mm (size 11 U.S.) or size to obtain gauge

◆ Tapestry needle

GAUGE

◆ 10sts/14 rows = 4"/10cm in pattern

FINISHED MEASUREMENTS

◆ 4"/10cm wide x 17"/43cm circumference

◆ Note: Headband will stretch slightly.

SPECIAL STITCH

◆ Square-in-a-Square Pattern
  Worked over 10 sts
  Row 1: Knit across.
  Row 2: Purl across.
  Row 3: K1, p to last st, k.
  Row 4: P1, k to last st, p.
  Row 5: K1, p2, k4, p2, knit last st.
  Row 6: P1, k2, p4, k2, p last st.
  Rep Rows 5 and 6 two more times, then rep Rows 3 and 4.

instructions

CO 10 sts.

Work Square-in-a-Square pattern, repeating the pattern 4 times or until desired length is reached. BO.

FINISHING

With tapestry needle, use Kitchener stitch (page 119) to join the CO and BO edges together. Weave in ends.

BASIC STITCHES &TECHNIQUES

Sometimes even advanced knitters need a little reminder. Here are a few of the most frequently used techniques and stitches in *Chunky Knits*.

Casting On

SLIP KNOT

A slip knot is the very first loop you'll make when you begin a project. It's also counted as the first cast-on stitch. Here's how to make one:

Wrap yarn around your pointer and middle fingers, forming a circle and leaving a long tail.

Open up your fingers and pull the long tail across the bottom of the circle. Secure the edge of the tail with your thumb and pull up on the tail through the center of the circle with the other hand.

Slip that loop onto your needle and pull taut.

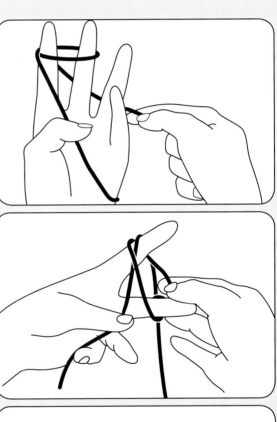

LONG-TAIL METHOD

Make a slipknot and place it on the needle, leaving a tail long enough to cast on the required amount of stitches.

Use your thumb and pointer finger to hold the two yarn ends open, forming a triangle shape.

Insert the needle up through the loop around your thumb, then over the yarn that's wrapped around your index finger. Bring that yarn through the loop on your thumb.

Drop the loop and pull taut.

Repeat until you have casted on the desired number of stitches.

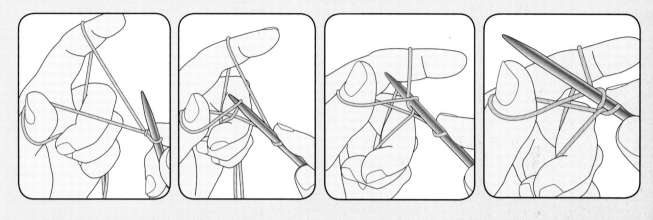

KNITTED-ON METHOD

Make a slipknot, leaving a 4"/10cm tail, and place it on your needle. *Insert needle into the first stitch knitwise. Wrap and pull the working yarn wrap through as if to knit. Pull the stitch onto the right needle, twist right needle clockwise, and insert left needle into the stitch so that stitch sits with its right leg in front of the needle and its left leg behind the needle. When twisted correctly, the right needle is already inserted to create another stitch; repeat from * until desired number of stitches have been cast on.

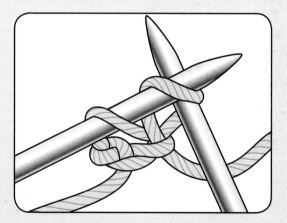

PROVISIONAL METHOD

The provisional method allows you to cast on, then go back and knit in the opposite direction from your original cast on row. The cast on stitches are not permanent.

With a crochet hook and scrap yarn, chain the number of cast-on stitches specified by the pattern, plus a couple extra.

Insert your knitting needle into the underside of the first chain (as opposed to the right side where you see the V shapes) and knit this stitch. Continue in this way until you've knitted the desired number of cast-on stitches.

Attach the project yarn and begin the pattern. The pattern instructions will tell you when to undo the provisional cast-on.

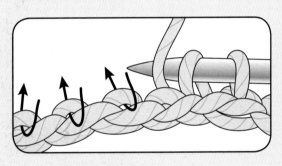

BACKWARDS LOOP METHOD

This method of casting on is most often used when you want to cast on stitches in the middle of a row.

Leaving a long tail, make a slip knot with yarn and place on the needle.

Wrap the working yarn around your thumb, holding the end of the yarn with your other fingers.

Insert the needle through the bottom of the loop. Tighten loop on the needle by tugging gently.

Continue until required amount of stitches have been cast on.

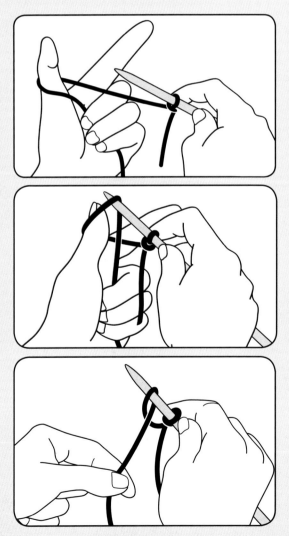

Decreases

SLIP, SLIP, KNIT (SSK)

The SSK decrease creates a decrease that causes stitches to slant toward the left.

Insert your right-hand needle into the next stitch just as you would if you were going to knit it, then slide that stitch right over to the right-hand needle. Repeat this again with the next st.

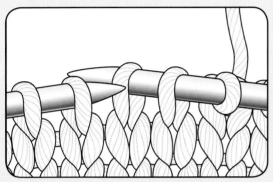

Take your left needle and put it through the front of the two stitches you just slipped. The left needle will be in front of the right needle.

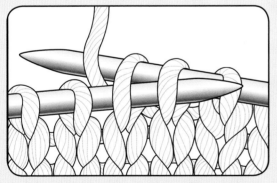

Knit those two stitches together, then drop the two stitches from the needle.

Knit Two Together (K2TOG)

KNIT TWO TOGETHER (K2TOG)

The k2tog decrease is simple; it's just knitting two stitches together as one. This creates a decrease that causes stitches to slant toward the right.

Insert the needle through both of the stitches and wrap the yarn around, as if you're knitting a normal knit stitch.

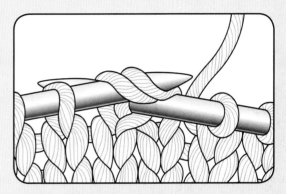

Increases

INC1 (MAKE 1 INCREASE)

This increase creates a whole new stitch between two existing knit stitches.

Insert your right-hand needle from front to back into the piece of yarn that is between the stitch you just knit and the stitch on your left-hand needle. Insert the left-hand needle into the stitch from front to back, transferring it from the right-hand needle. Knit into the back of the new stitch.

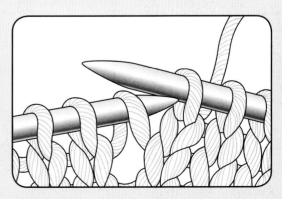

Binding Off

There are several different ways to bind off. Here are a few of the bind offs used in this book.

BIND OFF

Knit the first two stitches. Insert the end of your left-hand needle into the second stitch on the right-hand needle.

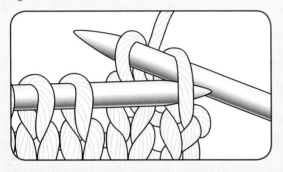

Pull the stitch over the first stitch on the needle and allow it to drop off.

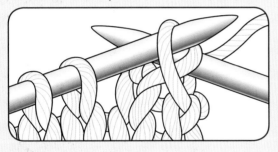

There is now one stitch remaining on the right-hand needle.

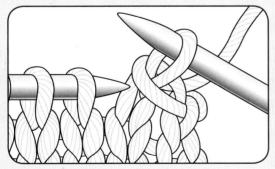

Repeat these steps until there is only one stitch left on the needle. Break the yarn, draw it through the loop of the last stitch, and secure.

THREE-NEEDLE BIND OFF

The three-needle bind off joins two pieces and binds off at the same time, eliminating the need to sew seams.

With right sides of the pieces together, hold both needles in your left hand. Use a third needle to knit one stitch from the front needle and one stitch from the back needle together at the same time.

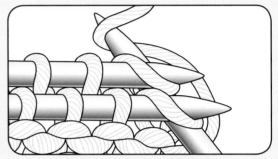

Repeat, knitting the next stitch from the front needle and the next stitch from the back needle together.

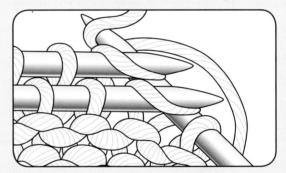

Pass the first stitch over the last stitch to bind off.

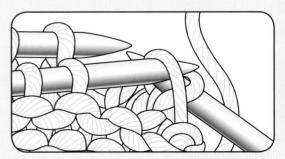

Repeat these steps until there is only one stitch left on the needle. Break the yarn, draw it through the loop of the last stitch, and secure.

Stitching Techniques

I-CORD

An I-cord is a narrow tube of knitting that's often used as a tie or tassel. You'll need two double pointed needles to knit the I-cord.

To make the I-cord, cast 3 stitches onto a double pointed needle. Do not turn the knitting as you normally would. Instead, slide the stitches to the other end of the double pointed needle. Bring the working yarn behind the cast-on stitches, pull tightly, and knit all three stitches using the other double pointed needle. Again, do not turn your work. Slide the stitches to the other end of the needle, pull the working yarn behind the cast-on stitches, and continue in this way. A small tube will begin to form.

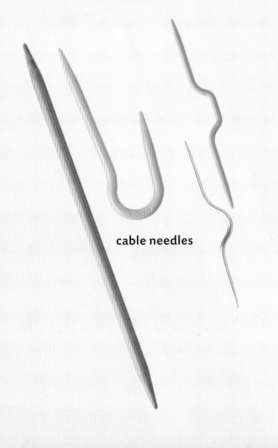

cable needles

CABLES

Those beautiful twisting cables you see in so many of this book's projects are much easier than they look. To make a cable, all you have to do is rearrange the stitches on your needle. That's where the cable needle comes in.

You'll see these two types of cable stitches used frequently throughout the projects. Master these and you'll be able to stitch any type of cable.

C4B (Cable 4 Back)

To make a C4B, slip 2 stitches to the cable needle and hold the cable needle to the back of the work.

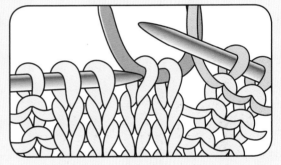

Knit 2 stitches from the left needle.

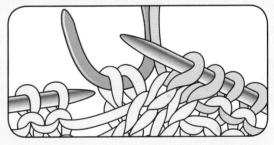

Knit the 2 stitches from the cable needle.

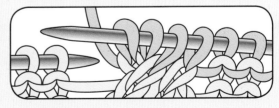

C4F (Cable 4 Front)

To make a C4F, slip 2 stitches to the cable needle and hold the cable needle to the front of the work.

Knit 2 stitches from the left needle, then knit the 2 stitches from the cable needle.

PICKING UP STITCHES

Some patterns require you to pick up stitches from a finished edge. You might do this if you're adding a decorative detail like a ruffle on a sweater hem or if you're adding a collar to the neck of a sweater. To do this on a horizontal edge, insert your needle into the center of a stitch. For a vertical edge, insert your needle between the running bar of the stitch. Wrap your yarn around the needle. Pull the yarn through, drawing up a loop onto your needle.

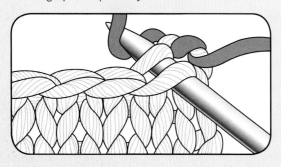

Continue in this way until you've picked up the required amount of stitches. Remember to space the stitches out evenly as you work.

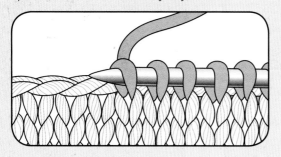

Crochet Stitches

Even though these patterns are for knitting, sometimes a crochet stitch is required to finish an edge. Here are a couple of crochet stitches used in this book.

CHAIN STITCH

Make a slip knot (page 112) and place it on the crochet hook. Wrap the yarn around the hook and pull through the slip knot. Wrap the yarn around the hook once more and pull through the loop on the hook. Continue in this way until you have completed the desired number of chains.

SINGLE CROCHET

Insert the crochet hook into the stitch. Wrap the yarn around the hook and pull through the stitch. Wrap the yarn around the hook again and pull through both loops on the hook.

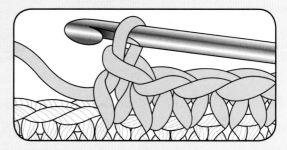

SLIP STITCH

Insert the crochet hook into the stitch. Wrap the yarn around the hook and pull through all loops on the hook. Continue until the desired number of slip stitches has been made.

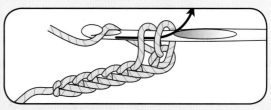

Finishing

MATTRESS STITCH

Place pieces to be seamed side-by-side, right sides facing you. With tapestry needle, insert needle under the first bar on the edge of one piece of fabric. Insert the needle under the first bar of the second piece of fabric. Continue in this way, matching the bars, until the entire seam has been completed.

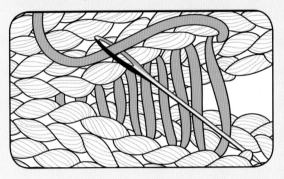

KITCHENER STITCH

This stitch, sometimes known as grafting, joins live stitches together for a nearly invisible seam. You'll often use the Kitchener stitch to seam projects such as sock toes and sweater hoods. Here's how:

Thread a tapestry needle with yarn. Hold the live-stitch edges parallel to each other. Insert the tapestry needle knitwise into the first stitch on the bottom right-hand corner. Pull the yarn through that stitch and drop it from the needle.

Insert the tapestry needle purlwise into the second stitch on the bottom needle. Without dropping that stitch from the needle, insert the tapestry needle through the first stitch on the top needle purlwise. Drop the stitch from the top needle.

Insert the tapestry needle into the second stitch on the top needle knitwise without dropping the stitch. Insert the tapestry needle knitwise into the next live stitch on the bottom needle, continuing in this way across the row.

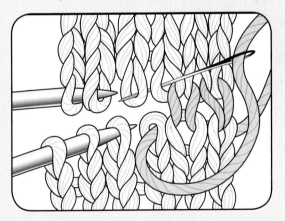

WHIPSTITCH

A whipstitch is an overcast stitch used to join two pieces together. To whipstitch, thread a tapestry needle with yarn. Place your two pieces wrong sides together and bring the needle through both pieces from back to front. Insert the needle into the back again and bring to the front. Continue across the edge to seam.

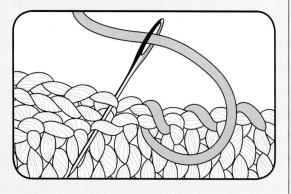

RUNNING STITCH

A running stitch is one of the most basic hand-sewing stitches used to seam two edges together. Thread a tapestry needle with yarn, then weave the needle in and out of the two pieces, keep stitches small and even.

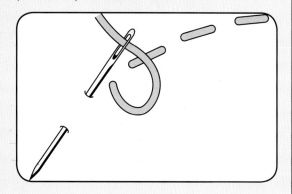

WEAVING IN ENDS

Once your project is complete, you can't just leave those yucky yarn ends hanging out everywhere. Use a tapestry needle to weave the tails in and out of your work on the wrong side. Weave the tail up and down, side to side, making sure it's secure and invisible. If your project has seams, weave the tail into the seams for ultimate invisibility.

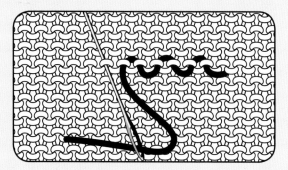

BLOCKING

Once your piece is finished, you'll want to block it to lock the stitches in place and give your piece the perfect shape. Remember that blocking only works on animal-based fibers, such as wool and alpaca.

Here's how to block your piece:

Wash your piece in lukewarm (not hot) water with a mild detergent. Lay the piece on a towel. Pull the piece into shape using the specified finished measurements, straightening the edges and any bumps. Let dry.

KNITTING ABBREVIATIONS

alt	alternate
approx	approximately
beg	begin/beginning
bet	between
BO	bind off
CC	contrasting color
cm	centimeter(s)
cn	cable needle
CO	cast on
cont	continue
dec	decrease
dpn	double pointed needle(s)
fl	front loop(s)
foll	follow/follows/following
g	gram
inc	increase/increases/increasing
k or K	knit
kwise	knitwise
k2tog	knit 2 stitches together
LH	left hand
lp(s)	loops
m	meter(s)
MC	main color
mm	millimeter(s)
M1	make 1 stitch
M1 p-st	make 1 purl stitch
oz	ounce(s)
p or P	purl
PM	place marker
pop	popcorn
prev	previous
psso	pass slipped stitch over
pwise	purlwise

p2tog	purl 2 stitches together
rem	remain/remaining
rep	repeat(s)
rev St st	reverse stockinette stitch
RH	right hand
rnd(s)	rounds
RS	right side
sk	skip
skp	slip, knit, pass stitch over—one stitch decreased
sk2p	slip 1, knit 2 together, pass slip stitch over the knit 2 together; 2 stiches have been decreased
sl	slip
sl st	slip stitch(es)
sl1k	slip 1 knitwise
sl1p	slip 1 purlwise
ssk	slip, slip, knit these 2 stitches together—a decrease
sssk	slip, slip, slip, knit 3 stitches together
st(s)	stitch(es)
St st	stockinette stitch/stocking stitch
tbl	through back loop
tog	together
w & t	wrap and turn
WS	wrong side
wyib	with yarn in back
wyif	with yarn in front
yd(s)	yard(s)
yfwd	yarn forward
yo	yarn over

KNITTING NEEDLE SIZE CHART

METRIC (MM)	U.S.	UK/CANADIAN
2.0	0	14
2.25	1	13
2.75	2	12
3.0	—	11
3.25	3	10
3.5	4	—
3.75	5	9
4.0	6	8
4.5	7	7
5.0	8	6
5.5	9	6
6.0	10	6
6.5	10½	6
7.0	—	2
7.5	—	1
8.0	11	0
9.0	13	00
10.0	15	000
12.0	17	—
16.0	19	—
19.0	35	—
25.0	50	—

YARN WEIGHT CHART

YARN WEIGHT SYMBOL + CATEGORIES	lace (0)	super fine (1)	fine (2)	light (3)	medium (4)	bulky (5)	super bulky (6)
TYPE OF YARNS IN CATEGORY	Fingering, 10-count crochet thread	Sock, Fingering, Baby	Sport, Baby	DK, Light, Worsted	Worsted, Afghan, Aran	Chunky, Craft, Rug	Bulky, Roving

Source: Craft Yarn Council of America's www.yarnstandards.com

DESIGNER BIOS

ERIN BLACK

Erin Black has been knitting and crocheting for over 25 years. She learned to love and appreciate yarn by ogling her Granny-made afghans and toques that arrived promptly every Christmas.

Erin uses her training in design and fine arts to update a traditional craft and create sculptural yarn art that translates seamlessly into classic and modern settings alike. With sketchbooks filled with designs, and not nearly enough hours in the day, her passion for creativity is never-ending. Erin's designs can be found at her website ErinBlacksDesigns.com, and her patterns are available on Etsy (ErinBlacksDesigns) and Ravelry (Erin Black).

CAROLINE BROOKE

Caroline Brooke doesn't remember how old she was when she first learned how to knit as a child in Ireland, but she does remember her mother patiently guiding her through numerous knitting and sewing projects for dolls. Those early

projects marked the beginning of what was to become a lifelong fascination with yarn, fabric, and all things creative. Now working as a designer and lecturer in London, Caroline continues to indulge her passion for creating knitwear. The full range of her work, which is inspired by nature and the beauty of the local environment of Richmond, England, where she now lives, can be viewed in her Etsy store, RichmondHillKnits.

MEREDITH CRAWFORD

Meredith Crawford is a self-taught knitter from Dallas, Texas. During the summer before her junior year of college, she decided to teach herself to knit, and experienced love at first stitch. She had no idea that a single ball of yarn could change

her life in so many ways. Blogging about knitting and crochet soon became her creative passion. She now shares unique craft projects, patterns, and yarn inspiration on her blog OneSheepishGirl.com.

VANESSA EWING

A designer at Plymouth Yarn Company, Vanessa Ewing grew up around the legs of her mother's knitting machine. At 9 years old, she began crocheting fuzzy monster purses and scarves for her friends. Vanessa's first designs as a teen were not real  patterns but concoctions of "sweater dreams" she had, where she rarely followed the rules. She holds a Bachelor's degree in fashion design with a minor in textiles, which has given her the design and construction background to achieve great-fitting, stylish knits. Her loving husband and sweet son Brennan support her in all her fiber-related schemes. See more of Vanessa's work at VanessaEwing.com.

JULIE FINOCCHIARO

Texture, color, and pattern are what excite Julie Finocchiaro about knitting. She believes knitting is more than just sweaters, scarves, and socks. Julie also uses the beautiful texture that knitting creates to add a cozy feeling to unexpected  places in the home. The lampshade covers and window valances in this book are just two examples of her knitting décor designs. Julie has been knitting for over 40 years and designing patterns for over 15 years. She especially loves creating designs using simple lace patterns that can be accomplished by knitters of all skill levels.

LYNN GARRETT (BISCUITSCOUT)

Lynn Garrett of Biscuitscout traded her city career in design and advertising for a slower life in the country town of Napier, South Africa, to work with her hands. Her love of all things handmade led her to take the old-fashioned craft of knitting and apply it to  modern décor and contemporary art. You can see more of Lynn's work in her Etsy shop, BiscuitScout. You can also connect with her at Facebook.com/BiscuitScout and on Twitter (@BiscuitScout).

MEGHAN JONES

Meghan Jones has a BFA in Fibers and Textiles. She teaches knitting classes at her local yarn store and designs knitting patterns full-time. Meghan lives and knits in Spokane, Washington. You can find more of her work at LittleNutmegProductions.com.

JOLEEN KRAFT

For Joleen Kraft, knitting and crocheting evolved from a hobby to an all-consuming passion that some would call an obsession. Inspiration for her designs is drawn from past travels, from Turkey  to Kyrgyzstan and many places in between. She dreams about wool during the long Canadian winters, often waking from her sleep with visions of knitting dancing in her head. She never leaves home without her handsome traveling companion Chris, a knitting project, trusty e-reader, and a picture of her slightly obese cat Ivan. Joleen's designs can be found at kraftling.ca.

ADRIENNE KREY

Adrienne Krey is a knit-wear designer, artist, and all-around maker of crafty things. She loves quirky, modern knits with interesting construction techniques in bold, bright colors. In 2010, she started her knit accessories line, Neeka Knits, which is carried in boutiques in Portland, Oregon, and online. You can find out more about her patterns and projects in her Etsy shop, NeekaKnits.

BRENDA LAVELL

After years working in healthcare administration and academic management in California's Silicon Valley, Brenda Lavell traded in her big city life and moved to a small town in rural Northern California. She founded her knitting design and hand-dyed yarn business Phydeaux Designs in 2008, working evenings and weekends in addition to her day job. Phydeaux is now Brenda's fulltime career and she loves commuting downstairs each morning to her kitchen dye studio. Brenda's hand-dyed yarn and knitting patterns are available online at shop.phydeauxdesigns.com. Brenda writes about her knitting, her yarn, and her new life at phydeaux-designs.com and obsesses further about knitting on Ravelry under username phydeaux.

MINDY LEWIS

Mindy Lewis has been crazy in love with knitting from the moment she picked up her first pair of knitting needles. While traveling with her husband, she taught herself to knit with the help of books and the internet. Mindy is continually discovering and mastering new skills and techniques, and she loves to work with cables and textures. She resides in southern Illinois with her husband and young daughter, knitting every chance she gets. Her designs and patterns can be found on her blog LewisKnits.blogspot.com. You can also find her on Ravelry as LewisKnits.

NGUYEN LE

Nguyen Le is the designer and maker behind Knitknit, a line of elegant and witty fiber jewelry and accessories. She also teaches crafts and is the author of 500 Fun Little Toys, a book of patterns and instructions on how to knit, crochet, sew, and felt toys. Nguyen has been making things since she was a kid. Originally from Lancaster, Pennsylvania, she currently lives and works from her studio in Brooklyn, New York.

AMANDA LILLEY

Amanda Lilley is a knitwear designer from northern New Hampshire. Amanda has tried her hand at many things, including playing the drums and snowboarding. Knitting, however, has become and remained her passion. She enjoys encouraging beginning knitters to challenge themselves and never stop learning. You can find more of her knitting patterns on Ravelry under her username, AmandaLilley.

MEGAN MANNELL

After years of crocheting, Megan Mannell learned how to knit from her mother at the age of 20. She survived her first few painstaking attempts to knit and purl, and within a few weeks she was the proud owner of a full-fledged knitting obsession. When Megan is not busy with a pair of knitting needles, she enjoys traveling with her husband, spending time with family (which includes two lovable canine mutts), and teaching high school English, currently at an international school in Honduras. You can find more of Megan's work at meganesass.etsy.com.

MARIA NÄSLUND

Maria loves thin yarn, small needles, and intricate patterning, but she was up for the challenge to translate this look to bulky yarns and big needles — and she may have found a new love. She finds that while bulky lace is not as airy. It produces interesting texture and can be every bit as beautiful, not to mention cozy and warm — something which is sorely needed during long, cold, Swedish winters. More of Maria's designs can be found at her site sticketyg.se and on Ravelry under her username marianaslund.

LIBBY SUMMERS

Libby Summers produces hand-knitted textiles that reflect her love for the colors of English and Scottish landscapes and the value she places on natural quality fibers. She was encouraged to set up her business when she befriended other women who were finding outlets for their creativity. At the outset, Libby's vision was to be a manufacturer as well as a designer and she realized her ambition when her unique hand-knitted hot water bottles went on sale in John Lewis in 2010. Her designs continue to get high profile attention, including being featured as The Financial Times #1 Valentine's Day gift in 2012. She has had numerous commissions from Artesano and Knitcrate, and her yarns and patterns appear regularly in UK knitting magazines. You can see more of Libby's work at LibbySummers.co.uk.

KATIE WORTHING

Katie Worthing knits and teaches art history in Portland, Maine, where she lives with her husband, Sam, and German Shorthaired Pointer, Arthur. She enjoys finding unusual ways to live with knitting on a daily basis and, as a result, is the knitter behind the customized Chuck Taylors at PrettySneakyShoes.com and an ever-increasing array of home décor items. In her spare time, Katie loves to collect vintage knitting patterns and plays goalie for a local ice hockey team.

ABOUT THE AUTHOR

Ashley Little is a writer and editor who left her job at Martha Stewart to freelance in the mountains of Asheville, North Carolina. She has her hands in all kinds of crafts, from knitting to crocheting and sewing. When she's not crafting, she's eating peanut butter, listening to Paul McCartney, and playing ukulele — sometimes all three at the same time. You can see what Ashley is making on her blog, TheFeistyRedhead.blogspot.com.

ACKNOWLEDGMENTS

Thank you to the talented contributors who helped me create this book of drool-worthy patterns. The process went so smoothly, and I can't thank all of you enough for your enthusiasm, cooperation, and all-around sweetness. We corresponded so much that I feel like I know all of you personally.

Thanks to my family, who I ditched many times to work on this book. I'm sure it seemed odd to buy things like knitting looms and yarn for a 7-year-old, but none of you ever blinked an eye when it was on my Christmas wishlist.

Thank you to the team at Lark: Amanda Carestio, who helped me develop the idea for this book from the beginning; Carol Barnao who designed these gorgeous pages — and especially to my editor, Beth Sweet, who not only guided me through the entire publishing process but also guided me through the challenges of office parking during construction. Thank you to Nancy Wood for her eagle-eye copy editing and to Cynthia Shaffer for her beautiful photography that made me want to crawl into the book and never leave.

My gratitude to Berroco, Brown Sheep Company, Knit Picks, Patons, and Plymouth for their generous yarn support.

Thank you to my Brooklyn friends, who released me back to the south so I could do things that make me happy, like write this book.

INDEX